I'm sure the Troubles must have made a huge difference to my life – it's just that the difference is almost impossible to identify. They've always been there, just on the edge. It's easy to become numb, almost to forget about them, to shut them out.

My childhood memories are not dominated by stories of death and sacrifice, but with bringing in the hay in the summer, riding in the back of my father's truck with the wind in my face as he left his workmate home. Endless Saturdays filled with making camps out of old furniture and having pretend high-speed chases with my brothers and sisters in my parents' abandoned Peugeot.

Of course I remember the helicopters scaring me when they flew too low, the soldiers looking in the kitchen window at breakfast one morning and continually being stopped on the roads. But I accepted these things as normal, as only a child who knows nothing else can. So while the Troubles never had a direct influence on my life, they were always there in the background.

Kate Fearon is political advisor to the Northern Ireland Women's Coalition and has also been associate director of the political think-tank Democratic Dialogue. She is the editor of two collections of essays: *Power, Politics, Positionings: Women in Northern Ireland*; and *Politics: The Next Generation*. Kate also wrote *Women's Work: the Story of the Northern Ireland Women's Coalition*.

Amanda Verlaque has been a journalist for six years and has written for newspapers and magazines both north and south of the Irish border. She is presently concentrating on script reading and working as a freelance unit publicist in Northern Ireland's growing film industry.

Lurgan Champagne

and other tales

Real-life stories from Northern Ireland

Kate Fearon and
Amanda Verlaque, editors

Livewire

First published by Livewire Books, The Women's Press Ltd, 2001
A member of the Namara Group
34 Great Sutton Street, London EC1V 0LQ
www.the-womens-press.com

British Library Cataloguing-in-Publication Data
A catalogue record for this book is available from the British Library.

ISBN 0 7043 4971 X

Typeset in 12/14pt Bembo by FiSH Books, London
Printed and bound in Great Britain by Cox & Wyman, Reading,
Berkshire

to Sadie and Hils; Eileen and Mickey;
and for Stephanie Grant

Acknowledgements

Many people gave generously of their time and advice in the production of this book. We'd like to especially thank our commissioning editor at The Women's Press, Kirsty Dunseath, for her thoughts on the many drafts and her patience with them. We should also acknowledge the many people who linked us up with many of the young women who have contributed to this book: Geralyn McNally, Lou Anne Martin, Vivienne McConvey, Goretti Horgan, Duane Farrell, Marie Smyth and Marie Therese McGivern. Organisations also helped, so we would like to thank: Edna Peden of Windsor Women's Centre; the Belfast Royal Academy; Greenway Women's Centre; and ChildLine. For those who offered us much encouragement when we were struggling we recognise Shannon O'Connell, Ann McCann, Hilary Donnan, and Bruce Coates.

Contents

Introduction		xi
What's It All About?		xiii
Lurgan Champagne	Laura	1
Footing the Bill	Stacey	9
Moving On	Lucy	13
One Cow of a Neighbour	Lorraine	18
The Twelfth	Rebecca	22
Part of the Community	Yee-Ling	26
The Wrath of Aunt Kate's Slipper	Sharon	29
Trauma and Truth	Kellie	32
Life in the Village	Laurie	37
The Way Things Are	Mairead	41
Travellers' Rights	Mary Ellen	45
Food for Thought	Caroline	48
Feathered Friends	Marie	57
A Passion for Politics	Vicki	61

Voluntary Work	Jenni	66
Sticks and Stones?	Rosinna	70
Different Strokes	Nanette	73
Out on the Town	Clare	77
The Best and Worst of Years	Katrina	81
Too Close for Comfort	Carol	87
Somebody Else's Conflict	Jillian	91
Jumping the Hurdles	Emma	96
Out and About	Sinead	107
A Local Girl at Heart	Jayne	112
University Challenge	Anna	116
What Next?	Bernadette	122

Introduction

This is a book written by young women growing up in Northern Ireland. In many respects, their experiences are the same as those of young women growing up anywhere in the western world – bullies and boyfriends, problems with parents, career choices, not to mention the demands of a hectic social life. But in other respects 'normality' has been different. As one contributor puts it, 'Normality is what you grow up with. Like seeing soldiers in my back yard was normal, or knowing people who were active in paramilitary organisations. Or wanting to look good.'

For some, the conflict has had a central role in shaping their experiences and beliefs – whether stealing the supplies that will make petrol bombs, being directly on the receiving end of sectarian hatred, or having to manage the long-term impact that a sudden death can have on a family. For others, the Troubles have just been a nuisance – not only do you have to look out for your parents when you go out drinking with your mates, you also run the risk of being caught by the police or army. The same thing goes if you are trying to conduct your first romance in the middle of a small rural town – if you've dealt with your parents and peers, you still have to contend with the army in camouflage.

Such experiences have helped to shape the identity of these women, yet the conflict has barely touched on the lives of others growing up in Northern Ireland. Many of these, particularly young Protestant women, speak of not thinking about their identity until they moved away from Northern Ireland at the age of eighteen or nineteen. And some young Catholic women describe how they only began to challenge the ideas handed down to them by their community when they were that bit older. Other women have had different priorities – being disabled, or Jewish, having an eating disorder, being taken into care, or caring for an unplanned child.

So ordinary adolescent experiences have been filtered through the conflict – sometimes in humorous, sometimes in harrowing fashion. But if the very different young women who have contributed to this collection have one thing in common, it is their practical, positive approach to life. No matter what life throws at them, they give as good as they get – even if it takes them a while, they get there in the end.

Young women, we discovered, are generally very busy. They have little time to write down their stories, and also tend to think their words are of little consequence. But we believe their stories are of much consequence, so we have recorded their tales, these tales that are seldom told, and hope you enjoy reading them as much as we have enjoyed putting them together.

Some contributors have chosen to use pseudonyms.

What's It All About?

Northern Ireland has a very long and complex history and any brief description of the political situation is bound to seem simplistic to those familiar with the issues. In putting together this anthology, however, we were aware that many people from outside the region don't really know what the conflict is about. To confuse them still further, Northern Ireland, or *Ulster* to some, has its own vocabulary; words and phrases that can leave anyone from outside the province feeling completely bewildered!

Most of the contributors in this anthology talk about issues that have a direct influence on their daily lives and, as we have said, the political situation is often only a background against which their own particular dramas are played out. But in order to understand their unique position, we feel it is important to give a short outline of some of the key ideas and concepts that colour the Northern Irish experience.

The main political division in Northern Ireland is between Nationalists and Unionists. Historically, *Nationalists* are mostly Catholic and believe that Northern Ireland should be joined to the Republic of Ireland to form a United Ireland. They can also be known as *Republicans*. *Unionists*, mostly Protestants, believe that Northern Ireland should remain part of the United Kingdom and because they are 'loyal' to the British monarchy, are also known as *Loyalists*.

The roots of both positions go way back in history. Settlers from Britain arrived in Ireland as early as the twelfth century but it wasn't until Queen Elizabeth I finally conquered the North in the seventeenth century that the *Plantation of Ulster* began. Because Ulster had put up powerful resistance to the British army, colonists from England, Scotland and Wales were offered large amounts of land to settle there – the idea being that this would help the British monarchy to keep control over the area. Many families came from Scotland to settle in the North, bringing with them their own Protestant religion. Over the following centuries, there were many rebellions by the native Irish against British rule, beginning with *The Great Rebellion of 1641*.

As part of a wider European war, on 12 July 1690, the Protestant William III – or William of Orange – defeated the Catholic forces of King James II at the *Battle of the Boyne*. 'The Twelfth' is still celebrated by most of the Protestant community today, with parades and marches by Loyalist organisations such as *The Orange Order*.

In 1801, the *Act of Union* abolished the Irish Parliament and bound Ireland and Britain together as part of the United Kingdom. A succession of movements attempted to overthrow the union, the most significant of which was the *Easter Rising* of 1916. The rising failed and its leaders were executed, creating a wave of sympathy for the Irish republicans. At that time most republicans were dedicated to overthrowing the union through physical force and the resulting War of Independence between Britain and the IRA led to the *Government of Ireland Act* in 1920 and the *Partition of Ireland* in 1921.

In the late nineteenth century, many Ulster Protestants had become concerned at the prospect of 'Home Rule' for Ireland because they feared their freedom and power would be restricted in a united, mainly Catholic Ireland. In 1912, 400,000 protestants signed the *Ulster Solemn League and Covenant* stating their desire to remain part of the Union. In recognition of their position, the 1920 Act split the 26 counties of Ireland into the independent Republic of Ireland, and the six counties of Ulster, which remained part of the United Kingdom. However the partition of Ireland overlooked the fact that there were many Nationalists still living in Northern Ireland who were against partition, and this sowed the seeds of the present conflict.

In 1967 the *Northern Ireland Civil Rights Association* was formed to demand changes in the political system because of the way it discriminated against Catholics. The campaign involved protests, marches, sit-ins and so on, and was mostly non-violent. However, tensions in Northern Ireland have always run high and some sectors of the Protestant community believed that the protests posed a real threat to the union with Britain. Violence erupted on the streets and it was feared that this would lead to all-out civil war. The starting point of '*The Troubles*', the violent conflict in Northern Ireland, is usually given as 1968. In 1969, the British government sent in troops to enforce order. These troops were initially welcomed by the Catholic community but when it became clear that they were to be a permanent fixture, they soon came to symbolise control by the British government, something Nationalists rejected. In 1969 the Provisional IRA was formed and it started its campaign of violence. In response, in August 1971 the British government introduced *internment* (imprisonment without trial), the aim supposedly being to control the violence. However, hundreds of Catholics were wrongly imprisoned and this both increased support for the IRA and resulted in an escalation of the bombings and killings.

The IRA is an illegal paramilitary group and both sides in the Northern Irish conflict have several paramilitary organisations (illegal armies) linked to them. Loyalist forces include the *Ulster Volunteer Force* (UVF), the *Ulster Defence Association* (UDA) and the *Ulster Freedom Fighters* (UFF). The other main Nationalist paramilitary group is the *Irish National Liberation Army* (INLA). However it is important to remember that the majority of people do not support violence and believe that the political process is the only way forward. This was reflected when the majority of the population voted in support of the *Good Friday Agreement*, made on 10 April 1998. In 1994, the main paramilitary organisations had called a ceasefire and this had led to a series of all-party talks. The Agreement allowed for the setting up of a *Northern Irish Assembly* – a type of government or Parliament specifically for Northern Ireland, with delegates elected from all sides of the community. It is hoped that by promoting a system based on cooperation between different viewpoints, Northern Ireland will be able to move on to a more peaceful future.

Laura Canning

Lurgan Champagne

Growing up here...nah, meant nothing really. We couldn't compare ourselves to other teenagers and feel oppressed and traumatised 'cos we lived where we did – we had nothing else to compare it to, so of course it seemed normal. The conflict was accepted as part of life, and we just got on with things without even knowing we were coping. Without even coping, 'cos there was nothing to cope with.

Being girls was a bit the same but in this case we knew we were coping. We knew that if we were caught fighting at school we'd get punished more than the blokes, and that some of us would get called dogs and ugly while no one would ever think of doing the same to the guys. But that was pretty much it; like growing up in Northern Ireland, we ignored it, we took it for granted, it was The Way Things Were, like poverty and air crashes and some babies being born with Down's Syndrome. So we just did what every other teenager did, male or female,

Irish or British or American or Australian — we smoked one cigarette between six of us, and drank cider, and snogged people, and hung around on street corners instigating minor episodes of petty crime which were small enough but which made us feel like daring outlaws at the time.

The only time we got caught was when we were out drinking, and it was one of those nights when we were 14 or 15 that summed up Northern Ireland for me. You take it for granted and you don't think about it, but every so often something will happen, maybe something minor, and it'll make you step outside yourself and see where you live the way other people must see it — like everyone staring at you open-mouthed when you're abroad and you've dived under the table because a car's backfired outside the pub... that sort of thing.

We used to drink every Saturday night. We'd all get a few quid pocket money, (some lucky sods got a fiver), and every penny of it went on booze and the split for ten cigarettes for the group. I was always the one who had to buy the booze 'cos I was the only one who could get served. So it was always me, going into the offy with a heap of sweaty coins to buy cans and cans of beer, bottles of cider, maybe a quarter bottle of vodka if it was someone's birthday, and the ubiquitous Buckfast tonic wine, aka Lurgan Champagne. More than guns, bombs and the marching season, the effects and popularity of Buckfast is something that can never be properly conveyed to those not from here. Lethal stuff.

I was having a two-litre bottle of cider, Cathy and Bernie were on the Buckfast brew, and Jackie, Tricia and Geraldine wanted beer. As usual I came out of the offy expecting someone to clap me on the shoulder and say, 'What do you think you're doing?' But it was fine — I got round the corner to where the others were waiting and handed out the drink to be stashed safely up sleeves and inside coats.

The problem now was where to drink. Those who'd designed our town had considerately left loads of fields and woods and deserted spots where decadent teens could drink themselves into a stupor in comfort and peace, but the more remote areas could get pretty lonely, if you know what I mean. We'd had lots of brilliant nights just by ourselves but it was good being part of a bigger group – maybe 20 of us sitting somewhere drinking. The downside was that big groups tended to drink fairly close to the estates, so there was more chance of being caught by a dad walking past at an inconvenient moment, or of a sour spoilsport calling the police. Then there was the additional problem of 'bog-breaks'. In the middle of nowhere you could wander for ages o'er hill and vale and have your pee in peace. In a group near houses there wasn't much choice and there was always the danger of some spotty oik following you and trying to get a glimpse of your arse.

In the end we decided that these were necessary evils for the crack of the big group, so off we trundled to the Bridge Inn, an embankment beside the bridge over our pathetic local stream, which we always misleadingly referred to as 'The River'.

The Bridge Inn was great – it was really ours. The walls were all graffitied, and not just the naff 'She Loves Him' stuff, but pictures sprayed in technicolor as a backdrop to jokes and quotes. There was also the legend 'Laura Canning Loves Gary Lennon' written in permanent marker by a callous mate who thought she was totally hilarious. When we arrived that night there were already about 10 other people drinking, so we found ourselves some space, spread our carrier bags on the ground and huddled into our jackets against the wall to start the night's festivities.

It was just another night until the police turned up.

Someone who'd walked past must have complained or else the police had been in the area anyway. It didn't matter – suddenly they were there, right in front of us and we hadn't even seen them. There was no getting away. One of them started to shout at us and Valerie burst into tears. We all started to think up our false names and hoped we wouldn't be lifted.

It was a game of roulette, giving false stats. If you were caught doing it, the police would definitely take you home for sure, but if you told them the truth they might lift you anyway. So usually some of us did, and some of us didn't. I said I was Sarah O'Neill and my date of birth was 1971. In the end the only one of us that didn't lie was Bernie, which must have begged the question of why a 14-year-old was drinking with a bunch of 18-year-olds – not to mention why a group of 18-year-olds were drinking al fresco in the cold when they could legitimately have been in a nice warm pub. But it was OK. The cops probably didn't believe us, but they must have decided they couldn't be bothered taking it further. All they did was make us open the booze that was sitting there and pour it into the River.

Valerie was still weeping Buckfast-induced tears and we were all embarrassed by her showing us up. Jackie was about to weep too but she managed to keep it in till the police told us to move on. The minute they left, she started bawling. We crowded round her while the blokes looked away and shuffled their collective feet. Jackie's mum was really ill with cancer and Jackie didn't want to upset her even more by turning up at home in a police car. She cried for ages before we calmed her down. We distracted her by talking about where we'd drink now, and we decided on Chinatown, the group of abandoned houses on the edge of another estate.

Most of the booze had been saved as it had been hidden in

bags or under coats, and the night was still young. There was an army patrol on the main road so we had to go to Chinatown the long way round 'cos getting caught again was the last thing we needed. That was the only thing the Troubles meant to us if we thought about it at all – there was more chance of getting caught. Teenagers in London didn't have to contend with armed soldiers coming at them as they were enjoying a Saturday night drink.

So we avoided the soldiers and pushed through the bushes. There was no way we'd be caught twice in one night, we reassured Jackie, who was still a bit sniffly. That would just be mad.

It *was* mad in the end. We'd only been settled for about 10 minutes when another police patrol turned up. We had to go through the same procedure of names and addresses and dates of birth, though this lot were a bit more cunning and asked us where we worked, so we were all a bit stressed trying to think up names of companies, especially as we were, by this stage, well on our way to being drunk.

That's definitely it now, we thought, once they'd gone. We'd never heard of anyone getting caught twice in one night, so even though the police had told us to move on we operated on the 'lightning never strikes twice' theory, and stayed put.

The theory turned out to be very, very wrong. Twenty minutes later an army patrol, very sneakily we thought, ambushed us, two from either end of the sheds and two more on each side. They didn't let us stay on the ground and slouch at them in arrogant teenager pose; they made us get up and brought us through the bushes where we nearly tripped over two more of them and where my coat got snagged on somebody's gun. Jackie and Paul were interrupted in their snog in one of the sheds (Jackie had recovered somewhat) and were made to come out as well, with Jackie loudly and drunkenly complaining that one of the soldiers had kicked over her lager.

This was getting a lot more serious. We were lined up like we were in front of a firing squad, blue offy bags at our feet, some of us still holding our drink. (I'd dropped my cider bottle in the shock of tripping over a bloke and his gun and was hoping it had landed in a lucky way and wasn't glugging itself out onto the dirt.) There was something about this time, though, that made us a bit scared and we all separately and secretly decided we weren't going to mess about with false stats.

So when I was asked my name and address I gave my real one, but still said I'd been born in 1971 – everybody else did the same. Tricia gave hers and then, brightly and tactlessly said, 'My cousin's a Brit as well' while we all looked at the ground, crossing our fingers and cursing her silently. Then they came to Jackie. She must have still been upset over her mum because she didn't give her real name. The trouble was she'd forgotten her false one. The few seconds' pause was the biggest giveaway ever, and she was so drunk by now that we could actually see her making one up.

'Marie Devlin' she said finally, and gave her address as number 924 in an estate that only had 800 houses. We crossed our fingers again and one of the soldiers went off to check the details that we'd given them.

We'd been through this procedure many times with both the police and the army, but this time seemed different. There was no banter, none of us saying, 'Oh, what's the big deal', and 'We're not doing any harm.' There weren't even any ticking offs or tuts. There was just dead silence. We looked at the ground and the soldiers looked at us and those of us still holding cans wondered if taking a gulp would be the final straw. Bernie lit up a cigarette and for once there was no clamouring of 'After you' or 'I called it' – it was just passed silently along the line.

The soldier came back and we knew right away.

'Which one of you said her name was Marie Devlin?' Our stomachs all dropped, like when you're really small and you've been caught doing something really big. None of us looked at Jackie and none of us looked at the soldier. We wouldn't have given her away and if he'd forgotten which one she was, she might have got away with it. But he looked at her and said, 'It was you, wasn't it?' Jackie ran.

It was one of those images you know you'll always remember and that, if it were photographed, would turn up on the front page of a newspaper – a drunken 14-year old girl running along a path, still holding her can of beer, and a man with a gun chasing after her. We took living in Northern Ireland for granted but at that moment I saw exactly how it might look to outsiders. Anything is normal when it's all you've known and you have nothing to compare it to, but something like that makes you realise that other people might be right; maybe we *did* have a lot to deal with and maybe growing up here *was* something that should be relevant and significant and slotted into our self-analysis. Here was my mate, she was 14, she was drunk and worried about her mum. And here was a soldier, chasing her 'cos she'd given him a false name. I thought about those teenagers in London.

He caught her easily enough. She was drunk and she smoked – we were all lazy and unfit. He grabbed her by the arm and brought her back over to the group. We all looked at the ground while he shouted at her for ages and Jackie started to cry – again. There was talk of being arrested and it being a Very Serious Offence to give false information. He was either genuinely angry or a very good actor. It went on for ages and Jackie kept on crying and we stood there angry and embarrassed for her, hoping she wouldn't get lifted.

She didn't. Fifteen minutes later it was all over. Our booze had been confiscated and we were told to move on and not to let them see us near there again. For a few seconds we just stood there, still in our firing squad line. Then we gathered around Jackie and tried to calm her down as best we could. She was hyperventilating from being upset and the booze wasn't helping. In the end Bernie took her home. The rest of us stood there, already recovering, already preparing to narrate the story to everyone at school on Monday. We'd been scared for a bit, but now it was funny.

And then I remembered my cider and I stumbled back into the bushes to look for it. It had survived.

Stacey

Footing the Bill

I grew up in Portadown, spending my formative years in what is geographically and politically known as mid-Ulster. But politics didn't interest me and geography was the stuff of double classes on Tuesdays and Thursdays. My life revolved around one thing: football.

I was always into sports: anything that seemed the slightest bit challenging and I was haring off to give it a go: hockey, kickboxing, canoeing. I was very much an outdoors kinda girl, but when it came to football, there were a few barriers, to say the least.

When I was only knee-high to a shin pad (I'm still only 21) it wasn't the done thing for a girl to play football. But I never let that stop me. Oblivious to social conditioning, I got stuck right in and played as well as – if not better than – the boys from my neighbourhood. Yet it's strange how gender segregation rears its ugly head. There I was, scoring goals left right and centre on our makeshift pitch, complete with goalposts made from a selection of jumpers and tracksuit bottoms and not a dickie bird was said; I was always one of the boys as long as I kept hitting the back of 'the net'. But was there a proper team I could join, maybe a junior league or an under-11 team? Of course not – I was a girl. Football was a boys' game, not for silly girls. It was a serious business, this kicking a ball about. But never mind, times were changing and I wasn't too pissed off. Why? Because there was a slow but steady growth in the number of young girls and women playing, and it wasn't long before proper women's teams and leagues started sprouting up throughout Ireland.

I suppose I should make a few things clear: I play women's football, not men's. I don't *want* to play men's football, because the two games are different in ways that matter: stamina, physique, and the speed and pace of the game. Men and women are biologically different, so it would be impossible to play men at men's football and expect a game of two halves. Equality on the pitch is not what it's about and that's what's nonsensical about the idea that women are trying to edge their way into the men's game, or men tackling women mercilessly when playing a friendly. What are they trying to prove, and more importantly, to whom? We're not trying to steal your ball! We just want access to some of the ludicrous amounts of cash that float around the men's game. If we had proper funding then men and women could both get on with doing their own thing.

Anyway, by the time I was in my teens, the women's game was really beginning to take off in Northern Ireland. Our season ran from May to September and we played mid-week rather than weekends. More women and young girls were playing than ever before and the 5-a-side team for which I played blossomed into an 11-a-side by the time I was 16. However, while progress was definitely being made, we still had to make do with a meagre budget and hand-me-down kits, which prompted lots of manic fund-raising by friends, family and people dedicated to the women's game.

I played at international level for the under-16 team and the under-18s when I started my A levels. A dearth of funding meant we still, for the most part, had finances amounting to a smidgen above zero, so we were unable to experience the opportunities the boys' international team had and never got the chance to compete overseas. In fact, the furthest we got was the south of Ireland. Even there we saw drastic differences in the international set-up. Money was being pumped into the women's game and their team was able to compete in the European Championships – something the girls in the North could only dream about. That's not to say our time playing was wasted or begrudged; it was worth it just to get out there and show what we could do.

During my A levels I found that all those years of living for football finally began to pay off in the most unexpected way. I knew that in America colleges were very serious about women's football and poured lots of money, coaching expertise and interest into the game. The coach of our international team recommended me to a number of colleges in the States, and I ended up being headhunted by three of them! I opted for the University of Southern Mississippi, where I now study Business Management on a full soccer scholarship.

Soccer in America is neither predominantly a men's or women's sport so there aren't the same gender divisions you find in other places – the women's game is even televised there. There are far more resources and facilities available, which enables the game to grow and players to develop their skills. At college, all of our equipment is issued to us – boots, shin guards, training gear and running shoes – and our away games are all-expenses-paid trips. This has been great because it has allowed me to fly to various parts of the US to compete, and see a little bit more of the country at the same time.

The women's game is taken seriously in the US and many individuals are working hard to ensure the game grows to a higher level. In Northern Ireland I don't think enhancing the women's soccer programme is at the top of any list. I know that there's a new centre for sporting excellence, which will hopefully mean a great leap forward for women's teams, and the growth in the number of female coaches is encouraging. I had to leave home to take my game seriously, but at least I was able to do that. I hope the growth of the sport in Northern Ireland means that the next generation of women players won't have to leave home but will have all the resources and support they need.

Lucy

Moving on

My name is Lucy. I am 17, and I am from North Belfast. My daddy was shot dead thirteen years ago when I was 4. He was doing voluntary work at a prayer group up in the Ardoyne chapel. It was Mrs Magee's turn to lock up that night but she was afraid because one of the leaders of the UVF or UDA[1] or something had been shot dead that day. They had already said that they were going to get revenge and Mrs Magee didn't want to lock up on her own. My daddy decided he would stay behind to help her.

They had locked up and were coming out the back entrance of the chapel to go home. There are lots of bushes around the chapel and in the dark you can't see anything because there are no lights at all round that way. The loyalists appeared out of nowhere and grabbed my daddy and Mrs

---

1 The Ulster Volunteer Force and the Ulster Defence Association. Both illegal loyalist paramilitary groups.

Magee. They tied her up with her tights and with my daddy's tie, and they took him into the priests' graveyard and shot him. There were police near the chapel at the time but they didn't come round till five minutes after the shooting. And that was it. He was dead.

It's been hard for my mummy. I've a brother, James, who's one year older than me, a younger sister, Anne, who was only three months old, and a younger brother, Tom, who was two. After my daddy was killed, my mummy depended on her family a lot. But then there was a big family split and that support just wasn't there any more.

For me, the worst thing was when everyone else at school was talking about their parents, saying 'Oh my daddy this and my daddy that', and I could only talk about my mummy. It was hard that way, but once you get to my age there are more people who have grown up that way, not just because of deaths but divorces and things like that.

I was one of the first ones in North Belfast to get help from a trauma group, although I thought I didn't need it. There was so much going on at the time, so many people being injured, that the group had to prioritise and only dealt with one type of trauma: death. I went there for about three years.

It was good at the start because Jane, our youth leader, was there and she organised everything that went on. She helped us through loads of stuff, even our GCSEs. We'd all more or less given up on them but Jane told us to start studying and really encouraged us through them.

We used to do lots of good stuff when the group first started up – we'd go out on trips and so on. We wanted it to be like a youth club and we even got a grant from the Lottery. But then the people on the management committee tried to pull back some of our money to give it to adults and that's when things changed. The figures didn't work out and the committee said we'd overspent the money. We hadn't, but we still got the blame for it. Young people get blamed for everything that goes wrong; at one stage they even told us we were using too much toilet roll!

When my daddy was shot dead my mummy swore that she would send us to mixed schools because she didn't want us growing up feeling bitter or wanting revenge. So we were sent to Belfast Royal Academy, an integrated school. Me and James have left now but Tom and Anne are still there. The school helped me a lot because you were mixing with Catholics and Protestants in the classes but also outside school too. We used to phone each other and go into town together. There was actually one point when my Protestant friends would come down to our area, even at night, and we'd all just run about together. It's not the same any more, partly because I was getting slagged off and called a Hun-lover[2] by my friend's brothers for running about with Prods.

I changed to a Catholic school after GCSEs and I noticed a big difference. In the Catholic school lots of people go round saying 'the Huns this and the Huns that', but whenever you are in school mixing with Protestants there is nothing like that – there's a bit of slagging goes on but that's as far as it goes. People go round saying stuff like 'they're all Orange b*******s' – but they're not. If they had the chance to meet some of them the way I've met them, five years of school, they'd get to know them properly.

But even though I did have good friends who were Protestants, it's still difficult not to get caught up in the everyday street politics. One day I was standing at the top of

_____

2 A derogatory term for Protestant.

the street with my brother and his two friends. There were groups of Protestants all coming up our street because that's where the buses park for football matches. This fella, he was completely drunk, came right up to me and said, 'Come on all you IRA bastards'. So my brother and his mates ran inside and locked the door, leaving me outside. I'm standing there, frozen to the spot, thinking, 'What am I going to do? Should I start running or should I stay put? What am I going to do here?' I didn't have time to decide. The guy came back up the street, spat on me, and then hit me a dig on the side of the head. I fell over and was nearly wetting myself I was so scared. There was a girl across the street and she'd seen what was happening and called me over. Once the wee lad heard her calling he went away.

I did go to the police. Our community's had a lot of problems with the police but Brian, our old community police officer, he was really, really sound. Brian went and found the person who hit me. The fella had his two front teeth missing, so he was easy to describe. Anyway, he'd been giving one of the policemen hassle at the match so they recognised who he was – they had pictures and were able to find him at the next match. He denied it, of course, so we had to go to court. When we got to court, he changed his mind and pleaded guilty and got 12 months community service, voluntary work or something, and that was it. Brian said to me, 'Put in for a claim, you're stupid if you don't,' so that I could claim damages. The way Brian treated me is the way you want to be treated by all policemen, but it doesn't always happen like that.

I remember another time, about two months ago, when there was another football match on, and I was walking down the street with a mate. A group of Protestants started on us, throwing glass bottles and all. So we started shouting things back at them. They were yelling 'Youse are Fenian whores', and 'Your ma's great in bed.' That sort of thing makes you want to shout back. So I took the mickey, I did. I knew that one wee lad's mummy was dead and I shouted at him 'Your ma was shot dead by an IRA man.' I know that's not a good thing to do, but you don't really think when you're in a situation like that. You just react.

There were peelers[3] out on the streets and they came over and started shouting at us for shouting at the boys, taking their side. It was so unfair – the police said nothing to the Protestants for throwing glass bottles at the two of us, two 15-year-old girls. Sometimes I think that when wee lads do something to you your best bet is to ignore them because that annoys them even more. But it's hard to do that, especially when there's so much discrimination against you and you've been through everything I've been through.

I don't think the Good Friday Agreement will change the discrimination or anything. No. There will always be some bitterness. It still gets to my mummy sometimes, especially over the Twelfth. She does her best, and she's been working with Protestants all her life, but after my daddy was shot, well, she gets bitter sometimes. I try not to, but it's hard.

---

3 Slang for the police.

Lorraine

One Cow of a Neighbour

There she stood with a hand on one hip and a fist in the air: my mammy. Arguing again with Mr Hughes, our next-door neighbour. Twenty minutes later the front door slammed and she marched up the hall shaking with anger and frustration.

'Bridie,' she called up the stairs, 'c'mere I want ye.' Bridie – my 4-year-old, bubbly eyed, freckle-faced sister – came slowly down the stairs.

'Yes Mammy?' she asked innocently.

'What did I tell ye about goin' into his garden and playin' with his gnomes?'

'Mammy, I didn't!...' Bridie started to reply, but as usual, mammy cut her off.

'Don't bloody lie to me, tell me the truth!'

'I didn't touch his wee men Mammy,' Bridie started to snivel, 'I was stealing his flowers.'

'Jesus Christ...I'm getting a bath, where's the flowers Bridie?' mammy asked.

'In the kitchen.'

'Well don't bloody stand there, put them in water. Lorraine, get a wee vase for her and help her love.'

'Alright,' I said, adding, 'what time are you going out?'

'In an hour.'

One hour later, mammy came into the living room: hair fixed, make-up on, excited and rearing to go. Our babysitter had already arrived and as usual Bridie and me were given the dos and don'ts of what we were allowed to do while she was out.

Mammy was going to a barn dance just outside Downpatrick and she was very excited. This night out had been planned months ago, right down to mammy and her friends arranging for a bus run to take them there. After we exchanged kisses she told us to be good and then left.

The next morning, I was awakened by my little sister doing a war dance up and down our bedroom.

'Lorraine! Quick! Come and see what mammy brought us back,' she squealed.

'Go away, I don't care,' I replied gruffly, pulling the duvet over my head.

'Lorraine, quick, please, come *on*,' implored Bridie. The child could hardly contain herself. She pulled and pulled at my arm. Reluctantly I got up and followed her sleepily into mammy's bedroom.

I smelt it before I saw it. A calf! Standing there on the bedroom floor! Bridie was trying to feed it leftovers from a Chinese takeaway that had obviously been brought back the night before.

Bridie's squeals had obviously woken Mammy; she sat up halfway in the bed and looked with disbelief at the calf. Rubbing her eyes (and spreading her mascara onto her cheeks in the process) she bellowed: 'Where did that come from?'

'Oh Mammy, can we keep it? It's lovely. We'll call it Billy,' Bridie babbled.

'No, we're not keeping it,' I said. 'And it's a cow, not a goat so you can't call it Billy.'

'Shut up both of you!' All three of us turned to look at the calf that was going to the toilet on the carpet with shameless ease.

'Shit!' cursed mammy.

'Very good!' I quipped.

'Get it out of here quick, put it out the back, hurry up,' she said.

'Will I take it out for a walk?' inquired the ever-hopeful Bridie.

'NO' replied Mammy and I in unison.

'Mammy, hurry up and get rid of it, my mates will be here soon and I'll be embarrassed and . . .'

'Shut up, Lorraine.'

Just then someone rapped at the door loudly and continuously. I looked out the window and there stood Mr Hughes, ranting and raving. Mammy jumped out of bed, pulled on her dressing gown and went to face the enemy.

'Are ye mad, woman? Can ye not leave me and my garden alone?' He was raving mad; his face was bright red and the veins in his neck looked as though they'd burst.

'What the hell are ye goin' on about now?' Mammy retorted, just as angrily.

★

He pointed to his garden. Mammy walked to the fence and peered over.

The face of every gnome had been painted black.

'It wasn't me, now piss off,' said Mammy, deciding that an insult was the best form of defence. She stomped into the house closing the door firmly behind her.

Mammy sat in the living room and all of a sudden memories of the previous night started to creep up on her. She and her mate Nuala were about to get on the bus to return home when they heard a wee calf crying. They found the calf all alone and, having had a few drinks too many, decided to bring it with them on the bus. Arriving in Belfast Mammy and Nuala tied a scarf around the calf's neck and brought it to our house: Mammy had been telling Nuala about her argument with Mr Hughes and they decided to seek revenge on his precious gnomes.

Now a very sober Mammy phoned the farmer who had held the barn dance; he would collect the calf that afternoon. Mammy meanwhile scrubbed the house to rid the place of the scent of calf's 'doings'. Our Bridie broke her heart when her begging to keep the animal fell on deaf ears. Personally, I was glad to see the smelly thing go.

Rebecca

The Twelfth

I come from the sticks as we say here — the middle of the countryside. I think that where you live does contribute to who you are. There are quite a few other things which form part of my identity — it's hard to pin down! As I've said, one of them is coming from a rural background. Another is that I'm a Presbyterian by religion and I have an Ulster–Scots background. Some of my words are Ulster–Scots, like 'bairn', which means 'child'. I don't use it all the time, but it certainly influences the way I speak. My family still have strong links to Scotland and we have relatives who live there. My family's ancestors actually came over with William of Orange, so I have a strong sense of those 300 years of history as well. My father, who was brought up in the Orange tradition, is a farmer. To him Orangeism is a cultural identity — he believes in civil rights and liberties for all. We work in a mixed community — in fact a mainly Nationalist community — and my father doesn't discriminate at all, he treats everyone fairly. So that's the background I grew up in.

Going to marches and parades around the Twelfth holiday is when all these elements of my background come together. When I was young, the marching season wasn't as exclusively Protestant, Orange and Unionist as it is now. I remember in particular that when we went to parades in Scarva on 13 July about 20–30 per cent of the people attending would be Catholics. A lot of people just went there for the atmosphere. That was in the days when Orangeism didn't seem such a political thing; the parades were more of a cultural event. It was like a huge pageant – like something you'd see in New Orleans.

Unfortunately the whole thing has become more politicised and some people use it as an excuse for sectarianism. But it wasn't like that for me at all.

This is what it was like for me: On the Eleventh night we would all go to a bonfire which local fellas had been building in the months running up to the Twelfth using wooden flats, assorted bits of old furniture and so on. After it was lit we would usually stand around with lots of other people from the area, a bit like Guy Fawkes Night. When the fire started to die down, we'd generally go to a friend's house and have a few drinks. Older people might go to a dance afterwards, but young ones would go and have a few swallies (I don't know whether or not that's Ulster-Scots as well – it means drinks). Next day – the Twelfth itself – it's up nice and early, about six o'clock. Mum used to get up even earlier to make the Ulster Fries.[1] For us it was a family day, all warm and exciting. The men's suits had been ironed and cleaned about a week beforehand, but we'd never take any photos until the Twelfth

---

1 A fried breakfast of sausages, bacon, eggs, soda bread, potato bread and so on.

morning. My mother and me, we'd line up my father and three brothers and snap away. It was like a wedding, a big ceremony we could all take part in. The planning of the parades usually starts two or three months beforehand: planning the route; deciding where to put up the decorations. It's a really exciting time.

I know people will probably be thinking, 'How can you be excited about something like this, something that's associated with Drumcree?'[2] The effect of Drumcree has spoiled things for a lot of people. It's spoiled the magic. For my wee brother, when he was younger, the Twelfth was his day – more so than Christmas. That's how important it was, and still is, for some people. The way I see it is that there's a lack of communication on both sides. Catholics see the parades as triumphalism – they see it as in-your-face, these Orangemen walking by their homes. For Protestants it's part of their cultural identity, they've done it for years, they love doing it, and many of them don't want to cause offence. My father and a lot of people like him fear, really fear, any trouble because it spoils their day. If someone gets hurt – whether Protestant or Catholic or a policeman or whatever – it just ruins it.

I have noticed that since the first big Drumcree protest took place, not as many Catholics have come along to the Thirteenth fair because, understandably, they're scared. I'm not talking thousands of people in general but the local people, who know and work with us throughout the rest of the year. They used to always come over, get a few pints in the beer tent, and have a bit

2 At Drumcree, the Portadown Orange Order wanted to march down the Garvaghy Road where the majority of residents were Catholic. The local residents objected and the police, the RUC, banned the march. The Unionists did not recognise the ban because they said it was a traditional route. Since then, Drumcree has become a major bone of contention and there have been confrontations and riots there every summer.

of crack.[3] It was a festival, just like St. Paddy's day, Christmas in July. I believe that Orangeism should be kept cultural, because that's what it is. I don't agree with any political party lifting it and using it for their own political means. I find that upsetting.

But to get back to celebrations. On 13 July, there's the Black parade – after the name of another Loyal Order, the Royal Black Institution. In August the Apprentice Boys, a Loyalist organisation formed after the Siege of Derry[4] march too. The other thing that happens on the Thirteenth is the Sham Fight.

The Sham Fight takes place to commemorate the victory of King Billy over King James at the River Boyne in 1690. The two sides – green and orange – are represented and they re-enact scenes from the Battle. The actors are local men, and they wear green and orange suits specially dyed for the occasion. This pageant was like a big carnival for me. It was fun.

Of course, with the passage of time Catholics and Protestants attach different meanings to the same events – they interpret them in different ways. I know that a lot of so-called 'history' is based on myth. I studied history, I know the facts – for example, this particular battle was part of a larger European War, but both sides have twisted it into saying, 'This is my part, my part of history.' In fact more Catholics fought on King William's side than on King James'! Most of the Dutch guards were Catholics – so really it was a European War being fought on Irish soil. But over time everyone has developed different views on what actually happened. And we get trapped in those views; we have to make sure that no one challenges them. In that way we are all prisoners of history.

---

3 Fun.
4 The Siege of Derry took place in 1689. For 15 weeks James II and his Catholic army surrounded the city. Thirteen Apprentice Boys had closed the city gates against them.

Yee-Ling

Part of the Community

The first question people often ask me is if I'm Chinese or Japanese. I tell them I'm from Newtownabbey. In terms of identity I see myself as Chinese – my mum and dad are Chinese, but I was born and bred here, so technically I'm Northern Irish. I think most people do understand that I can be from Northern Ireland and be Chinese as well. But some can be a little narrow-minded and I have to explain to them that I was probably born in the same hospital as them, and not somewhere like Hong Kong.

I am 17 and come from quite a large family. On my mum's side my relatives live nearby, but my dad's side of the family all live in England. My household is quite big because my granny and granddad live with us and I also have a brother and sister.

There is a strong sense of community among the Chinese here, and I have a role to play in that community. For example, on Sundays I go to Chinese school to learn the language (it's not my strong point!). There are also Chinese youth clubs but I tend to hang around with my schoolmates. My dad is vice-chair of the Chinese community and he helps to organise events such as the Chinese New Year party and various festivals. I enjoy taking part because it's good to learn about all the customs and festivities and what my life would be like if I lived in China. It helps me to feel attached. It's also good because our celebrations are open to everyone, regardless of race or religion.

Last year our New Year celebrations took place at the Waterfront Hall, a new concert venue on the River Lagan, and about 2000 people attended. It began with firecrackers and the traditional 'Lion Dance', which always gets the crowd excited. Then all the VIPs gave their speeches about how Northern Ireland was going to enforce the discrimination laws. Afterwards, Chinese musicians and acrobats gave performances, which were great fun to watch, and some of the younger children from the Chinese school sang for us. The atmosphere was not very formal although it was a formal occasion. The Chinese community here is very close-knit so everyone who attended the party was very friendly to each other.

Although I am proud of being involved, it does annoy me when people assume that I was not born in Northern Ireland. It's a kind of preconceived notion that borders on being racist. At school it's not like that; I'm not treated differently from the other pupils. I don't get or want special treatment; I just want to learn and enjoy myself the same as everyone else.

Although I do occasionally get racist remarks directed at me, it's not constant, but I can't speak for everyone. The community is very wide, spread throughout different areas of Northern Ireland, and the place you live in can affect how people react. I was in Belfast City centre recently with a group of friends and this one guy shouted, 'Oh look, there's a chink.' I turned and looked at him and thought, 'Well that's obvious!' My friends thought he was really sad and pathetic. Mind you, I think his friends felt the same because they walked behind him with their heads hung low as if they were ashamed of him too.

I suppose I feel that people should have moved on from old prejudices like that because the Chinese community is quite large – approximately 8000 people. The tension between Catholics and Protestants does take the focus away from racism, but every so often you're faced with these things. It's the same the whole world over – people look at you and judge you by what they see, and, for whatever reason, if you look a bit different they are afraid of you. They think, 'cos she's different, we'll single her out', but we're all people, human beings, first and foremost.

That's why I think that events like Chinese New Year are important – they educate people about different cultures. Every now and then the media will raise awareness of racial issues, but I think we need an ongoing campaign to encourage people to acknowledge and learn to accommodate a culture that is different to their own. And hopefully once they start accepting it, they will also begin to enjoy it too!

Sharon

The Wrath of Aunt Kate's Slipper

In the late spring and early summer of 1981, Irish history was beginning a new chapter. IRA prisoners in one of Northern Ireland's biggest jails, the Maze prison, had begun a hunger strike to protest about their right to be seen as political prisoners.[1] There was a lot of tension and rioting, especially in the streets of West Belfast where we lived. Being very young and very impressionable at the time, me, Brendy, Mackers, our Brian and Big Swanny (my two cousins) all felt we should play our part in what was going on — no matter how small it was.

After reporting for duty, my cousins and I were sent off to collect all the empty glass milk bottles we could find in New Barnsley, Moyard and Dermott Hill — our local housing estates. We had to take them up the mountain lane where a few

1 The 1981 hunger strikes resulted in the deaths of ten prisoners and an escalation in IRA violence.

young lads were making petrol bombs for a riot that evening at the top of the Whiterock Road.

After collecting all of the milk bottles from around the area we were given a job as lookouts. We had to shout 'Japs' to let the lads know if the army were approaching. But with me having the gift of the gab, we were all so busy yapping that we didn't notice the army coming up alongside Big Swanny. We shouted 'Japs' and started to run, but it was too late for the boys. In no time at all, Brendy, Mackers, Brian and Big Swanny were being frog-marched down the Loney[2] and through New Barnsley. Of course, the sight of four young lads (whose average age was 13) being marched through their own streets by the British Army provoked the local women and while they hurled verbal abuse the kids hurled whatever else they could find.

When the lads finally arrived at New Barnsley Barracks (which only had three holding cells) Mackers, Brendy and our big Swanny were each placed in a cell. Swanny's brother Brian (who thought he was the heart-throb of Dermott Hill but was now crying like a baby) was placed in the television room along with the Brits[3] who were watching TV.

The soldiers asked them their names and it wasn't long before an irate bunch of parents descended on the barracks. Brendy and Mackers' parents gave their sons a real chewing[4] when they got hold of them, and kept threatening what they were going to do with them once they got home.

Then in came my Uncle Joe and Aunt Kate. One of the soldiers pointed to the holding cell and said, 'Your son has been watching too many cop shows.' There was big Swanny

---

2 The Malone Road in Belfast.
3 The British Army.
4 Told them off.

30

lying stretched out – all six foot two of him on the bunk – telling them he was saying nothing until he saw his solicitor. Brian on the other hand was still crying like a baby. I think it was because he knew just what they were in for when they got home. Getting caught by the Army was nothing compared to the wrath of my Aunt Kate's slipper.

Such a hiding the pair of them got. They were grounded for a week, which soon put a stop to their bomb-making days. And after that, whenever they came into the house, my Aunt Kate was like a sniffer dog. The faintest whiff of petrol and out came the famous slipper!

Kellie

Trauma and Truth

I moved to Belfast a few years ago to begin a degree at Queen's University Belfast. If I hadn't, I would probably have stayed in the small town I grew up in, got married, had babies and been miserable for the rest of my life. Why am I speaking about my home town like this?

Well, for me there's nothing very attractive about it. It's a small village in County Armagh that resembles 'Hotel California' for most young people. It has all the problems of an inner city – unemployment, nothing to engage young people, problems of alcohol and drug abuse, teenage pregnancy, vandalism and violence – without any of the benefits. I suppose the village is quaint, maybe even pretty, to look at. It was originally built to serve the local linen mill that was very active in the late eighteenth and nineteenth centuries but was closed down about 20 years ago. As there's no other industry here, people either commute to work or don't work at all.

To me, it's an isolated limbo land; life seems to pass it by. Nothing impacts. Not even the conflict. There was a pub bomb in 1976 in which my grandfather on my mother's side lost the hearing in his left ear. The same year my other grandfather, along with two of my dad's cousins, were shot dead in their house three miles outside the town.

It was when I was just a year old and Mummy was pregnant with my sister Michelle. Some of the family were together for a birthday party – I'm not sure whose – when a knock came at the door; Auntie Kathleen opened it and three gunmen ran in. Granddad jumped up from his chair and said, 'Hang on boys, what's happening here?' and they just shot him. Then they shot my dad's cousins, riddling the walls with bullets. There were young kids there and from the newspaper reports (which I was able to read when I was older) it was a miracle none of them were shot as well.

No one was ever convicted of the murders but we've heard from reliable sources that it was a Loyalist gang. There were rumours that one of my dad's cousins was in the IRA. They were also Catholic farmers in a Protestant area. So it could have been land or politics or both. At the end of the day they were shot, they died, and we've had to live with the consequences ever since.

After the shooting Daddy had a nervous breakdown; I don't think he ever really recovered from the shock. He'd been working with one of the cousins on the oilrigs and they were due to head back to the Shetlands only a few days after the attack. Nobody ever got counselling and as a result my dad ended up leaving Northern Ireland and going to London. There were economic reasons too – it was during the eighties boom and Daddy was able to bring home lots of money. But I think that the deaths changed his personality; he seemed to lose his sense of responsibility, both for himself and for his family. After that, he and Mummy separated. If the killings hadn't happened I think we might still have been together. He's grown up a lot now, he's brilliant and I love him to bits. But it took him a long time – over twenty years. That's the way I see it anyway, the psychologists might tell you something different.

The shootings were never talked about in our house. I knew Granddad had been shot dead but I always thought the army had done it, I don't know why. When a knock came at the door, Mummy would always say, 'Don't open the door, never open the door.' The snib and chain were always kept on, which may not seem strange to some people, but in a housing estate where doors were either left open or keys were in the lock, it was.

Our town was comparatively OK, you see. It had two main housing estates: one Catholic and one Protestant and when I was younger there actually was a relatively peaceful coexistence between the two. So much so, in fact, that you would have a Catholic fella lighting the Eleventh night bonfire to commemorate the Battle of the Boyne and a Protestant lighting the one on 9 August to mark the anniversary of internment. To be honest, young people were more interested in drinking their heads off. There were a few 'blood and thunder' bands,[1] but the members also had Catholic mates and would take them to band parades and stuff. That wouldn't have gone down too well with some of their mates in Portadown, or other more extreme places, but in our town it was 'everybody in together'. It really should be highlighted as a beacon for cross-community understanding!

When I left school, I studied for my A levels at Armagh

---

1 Bands that played loyalist songs, some of which were sectarian.

College of Further and Higher Education and I loved it – hardly surprising, having been locked up in a Convent Grammar for five years. My subjects were English, history and politics. Surprisingly, despite the fact that members of my own family had been shot, politics were hardly ever discussed in our house at all. Of course, I wasn't completely naïve. I remember the hunger strikes,[2] although I must have been all of 5 or 6 years old at the time. I can also remember Thatcher and all that stuff – which surprises me because I was so young. Mind you, young kids are like sponges, they take a lot in.

Anyway, when I started my politics A level, it was like something lit up inside me. I saw the political situation here as war: Republicans against British rule, Loyalists against the uprising of Nationalism. The phrase 'The Troubles' upsets me greatly; I can't stand people talking about the situation like that because it puts such a nice veneer on it. People call it the Troubles in inverted commas because it's easier to talk about it that way than to say this is a war situation. People are living, dying, fighting for their rights. That to me is war.

And just as we can't seem to call the war a war, we also have a problem dealing with its aftermath: the trauma. We're a completely traumatised society, but we don't really know what that means. For these past 30 years we've had no idea what normality is (mind you, what is normality?). Without getting into a big philosophical discussion, I feel that we don't acknowledge our trauma because to acknowledge it means we have to do something about it. And that could mean having something like the Truth and Reconciliation Commission they have in South Africa. As much as it pains people to think about the past, I believe it needs to be

---

2 See page 29.

discussed, to be brought out into the open: 'I was wronged'; 'you were wronged'; 'I did wrong.'

People in Northern Ireland don't seem ready for that kind of discussion yet. Again, a veneer is put on it and we deal in statistics: 3000 people dead or 300 RUC[3] dead, or whatever it happens to be. We need to go beyond the statistics, to deal with the people who've been affected, to hear and acknowledge their stories. I mean, how can we expect people whose lives have been dramatically altered to feel part of a 'peace process' when they perceive they are being told by the new powers, 'Well, we're sorry about your loved one/what happened to you – now would you just shut up and let us get on with it', or 'Stop living in the past and let's look to the future'? I am young. Of course I want to look to the future. But as far as I'm concerned, this attitude is extremely short-sighted and unless these things are dealt with now, they will come back to haunt the north for years and years to come. The opportunity to acknowledge people's experiences of the conflict could be used to help us build a new society of tolerance and social inclusion. Hey, but what do I know?!

_____

3 Royal Ulster Constabulary – the police force.

Laurie

Life in the Village

I'm from an area in Belfast known as 'The Village'. If you travel into Belfast from the south by car or train, you'll pass the Village on your right side and see the Falls Road and Andersonstown, which are big Republican areas, on your left. The Village is 100 per cent Loyalist and Unionist. The other border of the Village is the Lisburn Road, which is a long road with lots of fancy shops at the top end, and lots of fast food chains at the other end nearest the city centre. On the other side of the Lisburn Road it's all very mixed – the area's close to Queen's University, and lots of students live there.

The Village has got rows and rows and rows of red brick terraced houses. A few are boarded up – it's a pity, because it would be better if they were all used. There are lots of gable walls with paramilitary murals on them, which adds a bit of colour. I don't really care one way or the other about the murals, but I know that if I went into a Nationalist area and saw the murals on their walls I'd probably be intimidated. So the reverse must be true also. It's not surprising that Nationalists hardly come into the Village at all.

A lot of people think it must be a mad place to live, but it's not – whatever you see on TV is blown way out of proportion. The media isn't interested in showing the good things. I've lived in the same area all my life – even when I moved out from my parents' house and got my own place, it was only across the street! I'm comfortable living here.

I chose to leave school when I was 16. I've worked in a jeweller's, on Care in the Community programmes, and now I'm doing some courses at my local women's centre, which is the other colourful thing in the Village. I also did some of my GCSEs again – maths and English.

I don't take much of an interest in the political situation – I think the less you know, the better sometimes. I went to an all-Protestant school, and that's how I see my self – as a Protestant. As for all this business of whether I want to be part of the United Kingdom or not, to be honest I really don't think about it that much.

My granny was a Catholic and she became a Protestant to marry my granda. That was at a time – the 1950s – when you could walk between the Falls and the Village without fear. She was by no means the only person that converted to get married but that was before the Troubles started in the 1970s – there aren't as many mixed marriages now. The mad thing is that I do have blood relatives who live up the Falls, but I've never seen them. My uncle died about three years ago and some of my other uncles came down here to the Village for the funeral, but I didn't go so I didn't meet them. I suppose we are a divided family – some of us, Protestant, living this side of the motorway, and all the others, Catholic, living across six lanes of concrete. It's not something I think about much and no one here ever talks about it.

I have been on some cross-community trips, when I was younger. I remember one to Donegal – it was brilliant. The other group was from the Falls Road and they were really friendly. When we got back home, one of the wee fellas took it upon himself to call round at my house. The fellas from the Village saw him and started chasing him because they knew where he'd come from. It's not difficult – if someone comes into the Village (he had cycled over on his kid brother's bike) you can see if they come from across the motorway, and that means they are Catholic. My daddy had to put this wee lad into the car and bring him home. By the same token, we couldn't go right up to his house. We just left him off at the corner of his park because we wouldn't go in, even if we were in a car. It was terrible.

Cross-community trips are enjoyable, but the problem is that when you come back you can't really stay friends unless you live in a nice middle-class area that's mixed – then I think you'd have a chance. When you live in an area like the Village, and they live in an area like the Falls Road, it just isn't possible.

I describe myself as British, though I couldn't say what that means exactly. I suppose it's a way of saying that I'm not Irish. When I'm abroad, I always say I'm British, even though everyone, even other British people, call me Irish. When you say 'I'm not, I'm British', they get embarrassed because they don't expect it. And I do vote, even though I don't get into politics too much – I think it's important to vote. Everyone here had a chance to vote on the Good Friday Agreement. There was an information booklet posted to every house in the province but it was too hard to read – you'd have needed a dictionary for every second word. It was very confusing for most people. I listened to the politicians on the television because they talked in a way I could understand, and in the end I thought it would be better to vote against it.

But that sort of thing doesn't make up a great deal of what I think or talk about – me and my mates spend much more time talking about the weekly biz, what's going on in the Village. And I am more interested in getting a career for myself, which is why I went back and did my GCSEs again. I'd like to be involved in social work. I'm doing a course in Women and Community Centre Management at the moment and I hope that will set me on the right road.

Mairead

The Way Things Are

When you grow up somewhere like the Ardoyne[1] you get used to all sorts of things. Like one time, me and my friends were up in my room and we looked out the window, and there were IRA snipers all round our back. We thought this was dead exciting, seeing all these people with guns and all. There we were, looking out the window, and this young fella went running down from Ardoyne Avenue, running down our street, and threw a couple of stones. He was shouting UVF[2] or something like that. The next minute this other man appeared with a gun and started shooting, just firing shots. I don't know what happened to the wee fella.

The boys[3] used to come in and snipe from our back garden quite a lot. They'd lie on our back wall and they even came

---

1 A predominantly Catholic housing estate in Belfast.
2 Ulster Volunteer Force – an illegal loyalist paramilitary group.
3 The IRA.

into the house. We just used to sit downstairs while they were upstairs sniping out the windows with their balaclavas on. There was nothing we could do about it – that's just the way things were.

It's funny what you get used to. Sometimes the Troubles even got you out of things. Like the time our school was petrol-bombed during the summer holidays. I was in Germany and heard about it on the radio – I was jumping for joy. But they hadn't done that much damage really – we just had to move out to these mobile huts for some classes. The Protestant kids used to threaten us, saying, 'We're going to burn your school down.' I'd say to them, 'Well this time would you do it right because I could do with some time off'.

In our school every single window had a grid on it because of the problems there'd been with Protestants throwing stones – it was like a jail. There was even a buzzer at the door. You were meant to press the buzzer and talk into this intercom thing. It was supposed to make us feel safe but the wee nun that opens the door just opened it for anyone. She was a bit senile. You expect to just sit comfortably in school and not have to worry about stuff like that. But we did worry.

When it's just people calling you names and things, you can usually laugh about it. Me and my friends used to get the Ardoyne bus up to school and every Monday there was this wee granny at the Post Office. She'd run over and bang on the window of the bus when it stopped at the traffic lights, screaming, 'You wee fenian[4] bastards'. We just used to laugh and go, 'Ach, shut up you oule bag'. There were other vicious grannies too. There was this match between Cliftonville and Linfield at Windsor Park. Most of Cliftonville's supporters are

---

4 Derogatory term for Catholic.

42

Catholic and most of Linfield's are Protestant so things could get a bit mad. Well, this match was going to be up at Linfield's grounds and as we walked up all the grannies were out in the street singing 'The Sash' and 'God Save the Queen' at us! That's like having my granny singing 'Up the Queen' or something at a load of Protestants. Worse even. But the oule dolls were so ridiculous, we just laughed.

You couldn't laugh as easily at the wee lads, though. I hated them. I remember walking through this Protestant area once, and one of them came up to me and said, 'You see – the next time you walk through here I'm going to pull your earrings out'. I suppose it could've been worse. But we always had to be careful about walking through areas that weren't our own.

It wasn't until people in my own family got killed that things got really bad. That's when I started to understand what it was all about. Like I said, it's weird what you can get used to. One of my uncles had been shot about eight different times but it didn't seem out of the ordinary to me. My granny had been shot as well – she was the first woman ever to be caught in the crossfire. She was shot in the chin.

Then there was a real tragedy. My uncle was beaten to death on 5 March about three or four years ago. It was in my third year at secondary school and I can remember the date because it was one of my best friends' birthdays. She called for me in the morning and I had her card and all waiting for her. She said to me, 'Are you not going to school?' I said, 'No, somebody was beat last night. My daddy thinks it's my uncle.' I just knew it was going to be him. I said to Rosinna, 'I know it's him'. We found out later that day. My daddy and all my uncles went over to Bundoran to identify the body, and it was him – my daddy's wee brother, Uncle Tony. He'd been living in Bundoran, a seaside town in Donegal, about a hundred and fifty miles west of Belfast, right on the other coast in fact – to try to escape from an INLA[5] feud.

What happens is that when these groups split, they start fighting among themselves and things can get out of hand. My uncle's group had split and some people were out to kill him. They followed him down to Bundoran and beat him up. It would have been better if he'd been shot, because the beating he got was awful. That might sound terrible but it's true. They wouldn't even open the coffin because he was beaten that badly. The family brought the body back up to Belfast, to the Ardoyne. Then, on top of that, about three months later his son, my cousin, was shot dead in Turf Lodge because of another feud.

It was awful hard for my aunt, Maeve, because she had baby twins. It was their birthday on 21 March and their daddy was killed on 5 March. The whole thing turned my aunt really hard. And even though we knew we had to support her, it was difficult.

Well, that's me, that's my story I suppose. There are things you think are normal but then something comes along and shakes you up inside. It makes you realise what's really going on.

5 Irish National Liberation Army – an illegal Republican paramilitary group.

Mary Ellen

Travellers' Rights

I am a Traveller and I've lived on this site outside Belfast for eight years now. The site itself is about nine years old. Before that Travellers lived in the Markets area near the city centre but they were getting hassled by people throwing stones at the caravans, so they moved to another estate, Poleglass, on the outskirts of the city. People didn't want them staying on Poleglass either so they were soon chased away from there too. They saw this big waste space here and settled on it, and the man who owned the land never bothered them.

There used to be about twenty-one families on the site but it's down to six now. Most of the families living here have kids but there aren't any play facilities for them so there's an afterschools project, which gives them something to do when they get home, like learning woodwork skills in the workshop or doing their homework.

Everyone has a Portaloo at the bottom of the site so at least each family has its own toilet, but we've only got cold running water and the tap is outside. That means if we want hot water we have to go outside and get it, and then boil it, which makes household chores difficult and miserable. The problem is there's no money around to improve things so we just have to make do.

I'd much prefer to get a house, but it's very hard. Before I moved here I lived in a house in Dungannon (about 40 miles west of Belfast) with my family. This kind of life has taken a bit of getting used to. I put in for a housing executive house about five years ago but nothing's happened.

There's not a lot of work for people who live on the site. Some deal in scrap metal, a traditional way for a Traveller to earn a living, but most people are on the dole. There's still a lot of prejudice about Travellers and it means that when you try to get a job, you just get turned down every time. It's demoralising. Once someone finds out that you're a Traveller the door closes. It's not just when you're looking for a job either. We were trying to buy a TV and video on credit a couple of weeks back and when the shop found out we were Travellers they called the whole lot off. That sort of thing wears you down.

Now, saying that, not everyone is as bad. Some have moved on in their opinions and, on the whole, people are grand. When I went to school in Dungannon I was treated the same as everyone else and it's like that for the wee girls here on the site – they're always chattering on about their friends from school and what they've done that day.

The new Human Rights Legislation should have some good effects for us. Also, under the Race Relations Order we're now recognised as an ethnic minority, so people aren't allowed to discriminate against us just because we're Travellers.

Being recognised as an ethnic minority should help people understand that we've got our own traditions and culture.

Really we do a lot of things the same way as everyone else but a few things are different. For example, when someone dies, the tombstone isn't placed on the grave until a year later and then families come from all over, a bit like a get together. Travellers used to have arranged weddings, but not any more. Also, when it comes to weddings, we don't send out invitations but that is because we want everybody to come along – we're not excluding anyone. Travellers understand each other and we keep to ourselves a lot of the time, look after each other, but it's all beginning to change and some people just want to look after themselves. That is why I think it's important to remind ourselves of our culture and our past.

There is a Travellers' project, which has been going for over ten years and receives funding. I work in the project offices, planning sessions on arts and crafts and trips away. It's a good way for younger kids to learn about their heritage, especially as our way of life is changing, and I'm proud to be part of keeping our traditions alive.

Caroline

Food for Thought

I come from South Armagh, which is a very small rural place on the border with the South – the Republic of Ireland. Where I grew up there weren't many houses, and only a corner shop. It was the middle of nowhere, really. The area was usually called 'Bandit Country' in the media because it was a place associated with violent Republicanism, and many people had been killed there during the conflict. But when I grew up I had no sense of fear – even now that I live in Belfast I go anywhere I feel like going and don't feel afraid. Like everywhere else, normality is what you grow up with. Like seeing soldiers in my back yard was normal, or knowing people who were active in paramilitary organisations. Or wanting to look good.

I suppose my story starts at my first primary school, when I was put into the remedial class at the age of 7. I was in a special reading group by myself – I'd love to meet the teacher who did that to me, who put me in that class, just to give her a knowing look – what she did gave me a complex for years to come. I had a real sense of not being very good at anything, so I saw secondary school as a second chance. In secondary school, then, I had to be perfect. I felt I had to prove myself, but it's only when I look back now that I can see this. I was constantly comparing myself to other people. I was never fat, I was always skinny, but I just looked in the mirror and didn't like what I saw.

At the end of my fourth year I went to the Gaeltacht.[1] You're supposed to go to learn Irish but I went to lose weight. It was easy not to eat there, as there were no parents checking up on you, and the people who cooked didn't know how much you ate normally. I virtually didn't eat for the whole three weeks. There was a lot of walking and dancing, so I was exercising too. When I came back I had lost a drastic amount of weight. I don't know quite how much because I hadn't been weighing myself beforehand.

I never actually intended not eating when I got home, I just found it hard. It all developed from there – an increased exercise regime, skipping meals . . . I just concentrated on food. For about two years running I had started New Year resolutions to lose weight, to look good, but could never keep them. Then Lent would come, which gave you another chance – it's OK not to eat during Lent – nobody passes any remarks. And there were always occasions to make special efforts for, like birthdays. So my parents were kind of used to me trying to lose weight, even though I was only a size 8.

I had a school formal coming up when I came back from

1 Summer schools usually found in County Donegal where children from all over the North stay in the homes of Gaelic speaking residents, learn the Irish language and immerse themselves in Irish culture.

the Gaeltacht so I went shopping with my mum for a dress. It had been a while since she had seen me getting changed and when she saw my body she looked scared, but I was able to make excuses.

Then, after the school formal, which was at end of September, my friends started noticing. I kept getting really cold at school. They told my form teacher who was so worried she called my parents in. Again, I managed to talk them out of believing I had a problem. I told them I had just decided to lose a bit of weight and they were making a big deal out of nothing. I insisted they should leave the doctors out of it.

Then, over Christmas I got really bad. I managed to put my entire Christmas dinner on my sister's plate, so she ended up eating two. The subterfuge comes naturally: if someone said to me now, go and sit at a table and pretend that you've eaten every crumb, I couldn't do it. But I could then. It was just something that I developed an ability to do. There were all kinds of techniques, like asking, 'Do you want to taste such and such?' And they'd say yes, take it, look away and then you'd put the whole portion on their plate. Nobody would notice.

But they did notice the weight loss. Despite my protests, I was put on a waiting list to see a doctor. The appointment came up immediately after Christmas but somehow I convinced Mum that I didn't need to go, and promised her that I'd get better myself. I still didn't think that I had a problem, just that everyone was making a big deal out of it. At that stage the only clothes that would fit me were for 7- to 8-year-olds. I was 15.

I started blacking out. My hair was falling out in clumps, my eyebrow hair fell out, and my nails broke. My face sank in. It got dark all around the jaw line and under my eyes, all motley. There were craters under my cheekbones; the skin was quite literally hanging off. But even though I must have looked awful, I didn't care. The only thing that mattered was my weight.

I started seeing the doctor. Every week I had to get weighed – when they started I was five stone. I went up to five and a half but then I started to lose weight again. I had blood taken to check the amount of white cells, went to a psychiatrist once a week and to a counsellor whenever I needed.

During that time I couldn't eat at all. I was afraid of food. I wouldn't walk through a kitchen because I could imagine food getting into my body without me controlling it. I wouldn't smell food. I felt fat if I drank water. I was afraid that if I took water there'd be something in it – orange juice or something. I was taking a lot of iron tablets but I even began to skip them because I was afraid that they had calories. I was eventually taken out of school in the spring because my weight had fallen below four and a half stone.

That's when I copped myself on – I had nothing. I wasn't allowed to go horse riding any more, or swimming. I didn't want to see my friends. My mum had to take time off work to care for me because I was too unstable to be by myself. They didn't trust me not to exercise, or do stupid stuff like going for walks – it would have been dangerous because I was blacking out a lot. For a whole week, I didn't eat any food at all, though it's hard to remember. A lot of the time my memory wasn't so good. I had started by eliminating food groups. I would say to myself, 'That's the last day I'm gonna eat (say) carbohydrates (or proteins, or whatever).' And then I ended up with nothing left to eliminate. Nothing. I remember at that stage – around Easter – being really, really hungry and going to take a piece of bread. I started crying 'cos I couldn't. I was standing looking at it and I couldn't even pick it up. I went through phases of wanting to get better and then denial, saying, 'I'm fine. There's nothing wrong with me.'

I hated both the counsellor and the psychiatrist. The counsellor would just talk *at* me and the psychiatrist would ask why did I do this or that. The counsellor tried to make me talk, but I spent the whole time silent – an hour at a time staring out the window. There was a family meeting we had to go to on Fridays, the only time my dad could come, and I hated it. I wouldn't take part in any of the conversation.

I was an anti-Christ to live with. Dad was always away from home, and I gave my mum and my younger sister a really hard time. They knew I was sick but it can't have been easy. They were trying to help me but I just thought they were trying to get on my case.

My sister had started high school and a lot of her friends thought I had cancer – I looked that awful. She got to know a lot about the condition and was afraid I was going to die. Mum and Dad used to come into my room at night to make sure that I hadn't, and that frightened her. Parts of my body were turning black from the cold and I could have had a heart attack in my sleep because if I relaxed too much my body could have shut down completely. The areas around my jaw, under my eyes and my hands were almost permanently black now. The rest was a green colour. I developed very bad circulation, which I still have. Sometimes my hands would get really, really hot because the blood would be restricted for a while, then suddenly pump into them. They would be the only part of me with energy, and it would really tire me out.

Then I went down to four stone and was taken into the local hospital. I was supposed to go in on a long-term basis, but there was no specialist bed, so I couldn't. My first meal when I got out of the hospital was a piece of dry toast. I blacked out, because my body couldn't cope with it. My mum kept saying, 'Caroline, you're going to have to try this. This has gone on long enough. I'm going to make you eat this, I'm not leaving the kitchen until you do.' And then she said 'If you don't eat this, you're going to die.' And I knew I was going to die, but it just didn't matter to me. Death didn't matter, anything rather than feel fat, or the guilt about eating. It's the worst feeling in the universe. I was ill, I felt pain, but the guilt is the worst, it eats you up. You get the idea in your head and it just tears you apart. But I did swallow that piece of bread, blacked out, and slept for a few hours to recover. Every piece of food after that was really, really hard. But I had to focus on what I wanted and recognise that I would feel guilty each time – I had to eat and learn to process the guilt. I knew it would happen.

My GCSE results were due out the following week. Mum and Dad didn't want me to get them because they were afraid that if they were bad I'd commit suicide or something. I had insisted on doing as many exams as I physically could. I wasn't allowed to study because that required energy but I managed to sit nearly all of them, although there were some I couldn't get out of bed for. A few times during term I'd be writing and my hand would suddenly fall to the desk, just stop because there was no blood flow to it, no energy supply. I used to just sit there until it came back because, for me, this was normal. The exam invigilator knew. I shouldn't really have been in school because their insurance wouldn't have covered them if I'd collapsed. The school were generally very good – pupils and teachers sent sympathy cards, get well cards and letters. One teacher in particular kept an eye on me during the exams. My mother would accompany me to the hall, but she wasn't allowed inside. So this teacher would go inside regularly and then come out and tell my mother how I was getting on.

Going back to school began to turn things around for me. If I'd had to stay in hospital I don't think I'd be here today. The professional medical help I got usually did nothing for me. The thing that helped me the most was Annie's group sessions. Annie is the woman who ran the Northern Ireland Eating Disorders Association, a voluntary group that provides support for sufferers and their families. They gave me the advice I needed. They would say, 'Caroline, if you're put in hospital this is what you've got to do to get out.' They were the only people who never judged me. There were even some teachers in school who used to say, 'Well, what do you expect, if you don't eat?' That sort of thing.

Mum and Dad heard about Annie's group through my local GP – he was actually OK, much more direct than the other doctors. He would say, 'Look Caroline you're not eating, what's the story? I know you don't want to be here, and I know you don't want to listen to me.' He was honest. The others, the 'professional professionals', had this attitude that 'If you draw, everything is going to be all right.' I was never the arty type. I never lifted a pen or pencil but they spent at least six months trying to get me to. And then they sent in this girl who was supposed to be a recovered anorexic and she was very big. She was tall, but big with it. She just scared me: was this what recovery meant – being that big? She also tried to tell me that drawing would help. It was just stuffed down my throat. A total dictatorship.

So me and Mum and Dad went to the group in Belfast. I didn't want to go, but I'm glad that I did. It gave me the chance to talk to people who had other eating disorders like bulimia. And my mum and dad and sister could talk to a relatives' group in another room. It was good for them because they had the opportunity to get it off their chests. I talked to Annie and a girl called Marie – she was training to be a psychologist, I think. She really helped me – I was able to tell her everything. She listened to me and treated me normally; it's difficult to describe but she just knew how to listen and didn't force anything on me. I'm not a very sociable person – my sister is much chattier – I'd rather stand back and listen. In the formal 'family group', the one organised by the doctors, I was supposed to tell these people all my problems and then walk out. I just couldn't.

My eating began to improve but it was very restricted. I was sent to a dietician and I had to write down everything that I ate. It didn't really work, but I did eat three set meals – breakfast, lunch and dinner – a day. I had to work at making the meals bigger, and tried to relax about doing it. It's only now, three years later, that I would say I'm eating normally. I still hate food and don't think I'll ever be OK with it. I analyse it too much. I just wish you could take a pill in the morning and that would do you, you wouldn't have to worry about eating. It depends on my mood now. If I'm under pressure I'll think about food; if I'm more relaxed I'll think less. Sometimes I can taste it, other times I have no sense of taste at all. Sometimes, it all tastes the same: horrible. And I know that's just me – what's in my head is overriding what it actually tastes like.

My weight did go up steadily, though it was really hard at the start, really heartbreaking. I was trying to put weight on, and nothing would stay on. I couldn't shop for clothes for a while and I still have a whole wardrobe to fit a 7- to 8-year-old. At first I couldn't do anything at school either. My friends would ring me, but I'd look at the phone and say, 'Tell them I'm not in.' Like I was out anywhere! I didn't want to talk to anybody. I just read and exercised a lot. I didn't have a boyfriend, but whenever I went back to school there was a guy, an old friend of the family. We might have gone out together, I knew he'd be on for it, but I just made him feel crap. I treated everybody so badly. I just didn't want anybody near me. I was really terrible to the people I cared about.

I cook for myself now, and I know from memory not to listen to my body. When I'm under pressure I can feel the first signs of slipping back. Not eating was like a haven I could crawl into – it was hell, but it's where I felt comfortable. I know myself better for having come through this. I can reason with myself now. I'm 18, I have great friends and I've never been happier.

Marie

Feathered Friends

I'd never been overseas; in fact I'd never been out of my parents' company for longer than the length of a school day. Amazingly, though, here I was seated opposite Mum and Dad and being told that I'd be spending three weeks of the summer in Holland – *without them*! I was 8 years old.

After this announcement, my mum sort of gingerly moved closer to me and took my hand – not bad news, I hoped. She began to tell me that I'd be travelling to Holland with about 30 other kids from all over Northern Ireland and that we'd be staying with different host families. Mine were called the Barrensdens. Not only that, but there would be another girl staying with them too – Kathleen from Londonderry, who was also 8 and (shock, horror) a Catholic.

Alarm bells started ringing; even at 8 years old our country's troubled history had already rubbed off on me. My parents weren't prejudiced so how could I have picked up on these attitudes so young? In retrospect I can only put it down to the images I saw on the news, of bombs and shootings, that showed how, if one person's religion differed from another's, they could somehow became a target. As a little girl I certainly didn't understand the politics involved. To me, it was simplified down to the idea that Protestants were supposed to hate Catholics and Catholics were supposed to hate Protestants.

I pondered this for a while – the thought of having to hate someone I'd never met concerned me more than the fact that I'd be spending three weeks away from my mum and dad in a different country with a bunch of strangers.

In no time at time, D-Day had arrived. My journey, my first ever journey, to the airport was filled with terror and the kind of excitement that only a child can feel. Once I'd waved a slightly tearful goodbye to my parents, I was ushered into a queue full of children, my travelling companions, and given a name badge. I was horrified to discover that the name on my badge was wrong. My name wasn't Mary, it was *Marie*. Details like that are important to an 8-year-old, and during my three weeks away, no matter how much I protested, the only person who got my name right was Kathleen.

Kathleen and I were introduced after the name badges had all been handed out. She was slightly taller than me, with darker hair and a cute bunch of freckles over her nose. We both smiled coyly and said Hello. I could tell she was as overwhelmed by the whole situation as I was, and my gut reaction at that time was that we were going to be great friends.

After what was literally the longest journey of our lives, Kathleen and I arrived wide-eyed at the home of the Barrensdens. They welcomed us with open and reassuring arms, and introduced themselves as Uncle Peter and Auntie Margaret. Their warm smiles claimed us immediately and their home was unlike anything I'd ever seen before – it was like a zoo. They had dogs, cats, fish, birds and at the end of their garden, they had chickens – fantastic! Kathleen and I were given the proud duty of checking the chicken pen each morning for freshly laid eggs.

The Barrensdens were a wonderful family who, along with their three grown-up children, treated us like princesses – we were spoilt rotten. And at first Kathleen and I got on like a house on fire, sharing an exciting adventure a long way from home. Then the fighting began.

It was very petty to begin with – arguments about who was the family's favourite, or who was going to collect the eggs – but then things got worse. Inevitably religion reared its ugly head and for a while we had a series of 'Dynasty'-style catfights, with 'Orange bitch' or 'Fenian bitch' preceding the hair pulling and eye scratching. It got so bad that Auntie Margaret and Uncle Peter were forced to call a crisis meeting. So there we sat, glaring at each other, as they told us they were no longer prepared to tolerate our behaviour and that we were on the verge of being sent home.

We'd been handed a wake-up call. I knew I didn't hate Kathleen and she didn't hate me. I couldn't care less that she was a Catholic and vice-versa, so why were we fighting? I guess, looking back, we fought because we both had the idea in the back of our minds that we were supposed to hate each other, but we just couldn't. After that we were the best of friends again. We had the odd petty squabble here and there, but we were kids and kids fall out all the time.

At the end of three weeks, saying goodbye to our host family was heartbreaking – we all wept buckets. But out of all the new people I had met during this adventure, I knew Kathleen was the one that I would miss the most. As we said even more tearful goodbyes at the airport, we promised to keep in touch. And we did, for a while, but kids being kids we soon moved on and I haven't heard from her since.

I firmly believe that certain people in your life help to colour and shape the way you treat others. I can never imagine myself discriminating against someone simply because they come from a different background than me. In fact I love it when opportunities arise for me to experience or learn a little bit more about different cultures and traditions. I've also spent time as a voluntary worker in a Women's Centre and when I meet new people there I never have the old alarm bells ringing! Instead I like to concentrate on what we might have in common instead of what our differences are. I truly believe that I feel and act this way because of the time I spent with Kathleen in Holland all those years ago. Our friendship helped to show me the futility of prejudice.

So Kathleen, thanks for being my friend and I hope you're well, wherever you are.

Vicki

A Passion for Politics

To some, I am extraordinary by my very ordinariness. Having grown up in Northern Ireland I have never had any first-hand experience of the violence that has made it so infamous. I was brought up in Newtownards, a predominantly Protestant, prosperous town ten miles from Belfast, and my life has been a lot easier than it has been for many people. I can't pretend to know what it's like to live in areas where the violence is on your doorstep, but I can't ignore it either. That's probably why I became involved in politics.

I first became politically aware when I was a student in England. Very few people there understood the Northern Irish conflict and I soon realised that I didn't either. Any attempt to explain it made it seem pointless and trivial but I knew that it was important to a lot of people back home. I wanted to be better informed about what was going on, but I needed to think carefully about my own views too. I had never felt particularly 'British' or 'Irish' and was more worried about things like unemployment and education – problems I could identify with.

When I came back from college, times had changed – major negotiations were about to take place on the future of Northern Ireland. So I decided to take the plunge and got involved with one of the newer political parties – the Northern Ireland Women's Coalition. I've always been opinionated, passionate about the things I believe in and now I wanted to channel my energy into something useful. The traditional political parties never offered me anything but here was a party made up of women doing politics for themselves. They were interested in what I thought as a young person, and they gave me the opportunity to make a contribution to my own future.

I found myself roped into the elections that were held to decide on who would represent the party at the negotiations – you can imagine how I felt when I was chosen as a candidate in my home constituency. The morning after, I woke up thinking, 'Oh my God! What have I done?' I really did panic and it took me about two weeks to tell my boss!

I was thrown in at the deep end. I found myself debating in the street with politicians who were much older and more experienced than myself (not to mention more male!). The local press was particularly interested, as I was so young, which I found a bit embarrassing at first. I was genuinely surprised when I stopped and realised what a good time I was having – it was exhausting and chaotic, but fun all the same. Some of my friends thought I was mad, but others were more supportive. The whole experience gave me so much confidence.

The night of the election results, I sat in a Belfast city centre pub with my mates, biting my nails, and listening to the radio.

When I realised the party had won the two seats we'd been aiming for I couldn't believe it. I was convinced from the beginning that we could do it, although I knew it was a tall order, but when it dawned on me that we actually *had*, it was amazing – I'll never forget that night.

There were other campaigns to follow – also hard work, but also successful. Two fingers up to the non-believers! You do get abuse from some people – I've been told I'm going to hell for talking to 'terrorists', been told I'm nothing but 'Sinn Fein in a skirt' (whatever that means), but sure, it makes for interesting conversations!

Through my continued involvement in politics, I had the opportunity to work in Washington DC, as an intern in the First Lady's Office. I met Mrs Clinton and she mentioned me in her speech during her trip to Northern Ireland in 1998. My mum even admitted to shedding a tear! A photograph of me shaking hands with the First Lady sits in our living room at home.

The United States' fascination with Northern Ireland overwhelmed me, as did their lack of understanding. Americans have amazing goodwill towards the peace process but unsurprisingly many don't really know a great deal about the country – I was even asked if we have computers in Ireland! My host family was great – they had been to Ireland and knew something of the political situation, and that it's a really beautiful place. It's great when people realise there is more to Northern Ireland than its problems.

Ironically, those I became closest to amongst the other interns from Ireland were, on the surface, very different from myself. Different background, different religion, different political party. Same concerns and beliefs. I did face criticism for my involvement in a newer party from interns with the older, more established ones, and I found it very hard to let it wash over me. I only realised afterwards that the criticism has strengthened me, made me more determined.

During my time in Washington I also became good friends with an American intern called Jennifer. She was Jewish and asked me were there any Jews living in Northern Ireland. I didn't really know, and was embarrassed that the political scene in Northern Ireland seems to have so little time for anything other than the conflict. She was interested in the situation, and I think what shocked her most was just how small the place actually is. The amount of air time and column space that Northern Ireland occupies, you'd think it was huge – some people think it's their whole world.

Before I went to the States, I'd always seen it as a successful, multicultural, democratic society but while I was there most of the people I met and mixed with were privileged and white. The only black people I saw were driving buses or working in the Post Office. I also found it hard to understand the political apathy among the young – but then they couldn't understand my passion for politics either. So my time in America helped me see it as a three-dimensional country – a place of enormous opportunities, of course, but with bigotry and tensions just like home.

The experience I gained there also taught me a great deal about myself. I'd always felt slightly embarrassed about being a Protestant, or maybe it was just outwardly admitting it. I'd always identified it with having a baby-eating, job-stealing image and was never comfortable with it. But I came to appreciate that my background is an important part of who I am.

As a young person I would like to increase youth involvement in the party. I see my role as a channel for young people within the party and outside it, feeding their views through to the decision-making level. I understand that not all young people want to become involved in politics, but the new Assembly has given us the scope to lobby our own government, to be heard, to have our needs met. We are the ones who can change things.

And so I've been smitten. I do have bad days, of course, but I know that I feel happy now, being totally immersed in politics. I always feel self-conscious when I go out and talk in public, but then I remind myself why I'm doing what I'm doing, that I really love it, and that I'm glad to be involved in something I'm proud of.

Jenni

Voluntary Work

At the moment I'm a full-time student studying psychology but what takes up a lot of my spare time is my voluntary work with ChildLine. ChildLine is a 24-hour confidential helpline for young people. It deals with all sorts of problems, from bullying to physical and sexual abuse. As I had always been interested in a career in social work or working with children, getting involved with ChildLine seemed like a really good idea – and to be honest, it was also because I needed something, some sort of voluntary work, for my CV!

Last year one of our local TV programmes carried some information on being a volunteer for the organisation. They mentioned that there would be a series of information meetings so I went along and filled in an application form. The following week I was told that I had an interview with the Northern Ireland Director of ChildLine. The interview was 45 minutes long and we touched on some really personal and emotive issues. I felt very nervous. When I heard that I was successful and was able to go on the training course, I was so pleased. I realised that doing this had become really important to me.

The training started in August and lasted for three months. After my final assessment they told me that I could now work as a voluntary counsellor. I was thrilled, of course, but as soon as I started doing it, I realised there's more, much more to it than meets the eye. It does take up a lot of your time and you need to be dedicated. But it has also taught me a lot, a whole range of skills: commitment, patience, learning to be non-judgemental and respectful of other people's contributions, and how to work as part of a team. I think I've become a better person for it.

I've now been fully trained for three months. The training was pretty intense and there were stages when I wasn't too sure if I would get through. You face a lot of things you probably don't experience in everyday life — hearing about things like sexual or physical abuse — so your whole value system changes. You don't take things for granted any more. You're certainly not as naïve or as ignorant to what's going on. I had a good family life, so until I started working for ChildLine, I'd only heard about things like this on TV. You have to distance yourself, of course, or you wouldn't be able to do your job, but the things you hear on your shift can be very shocking.

You normally do one four-hour shift per week but volunteers can do other shifts if they want to. Before you even go into the counselling room there is a fifteen minutes to half an hour briefing. This is followed by a three-hour shift on the phone where you're answering calls from young people, and then another half hour where you have a debrief and can talk about how you felt you coped, or if something really annoyed you or made you happy. It's basically an assessment of your shift. The full-time staff are extremely supportive.

ChildLine Northern Ireland was established in December 1999. We have a call centre in Belfast. Before that all the Northern Ireland calls went through the Manchester centre. It only had two lines that dealt with Northern Irish calls and there was something like an average of 5000 calls a week. 5000 calls a week in a population of 1.5 million people! And only a handful of those calls were getting answered, so there was a real need for a call centre here. We have 51 volunteers at present and the advice we can offer and the number of calls we can field is amazing. We still need more resources, but at least children are getting through now.

There are a lot of real issues here that tend to go unnoticed or are swept under the carpet. Although we deal with a whole range of problems, the biggest issues for callers seem to be bullying, and physical and sexual abuse. The political situation does to some extent influence the type of issues raised, especially when someone is the object of sectarian bullying for example (if it is based on religion then it's sectarian). Bullying is always difficult to deal with, especially when you're on the end of a phone. The only advice you can really offer is who kids can go and see, if that's what they want, and a listening ear. Sectarian bullying is mainly down to ignorance and fear because kids are wearing a particular school uniform or live in a particular area. But even though there may be wider community issues, we try to focus on the bullying itself, and how that's making the individual caller feel. That's the most important thing, to be caller-centred. It's important that callers feel they can actually say how they feel, and what they want to see happen, and, of course to find out how we can help them. We're not necessarily there to sort out all of their problems in one call, but to help them identify the options they have.

But not all the calls are serious in nature. We get calls from kids thanking us for something that went right on the advice of a counsellor or even just phoning up to say they had a good day. Maybe they've phoned before on a bad day and they just want to tell us that things are getting better. I do get a buzz from helping callers, listening to their problems and knowing they feel safe enough to talk to me. Working for ChildLine gives me a real sense of well-being. It's a way of helping an awful lot of young people as well.

Considering I originally went for this position to beef up my CV (in today's world everybody needs more than a degree to get a job!), it was amazing to find out how near-sighted I could be. My priorities have changed in a big way, and it helps to know that I'm committing myself to something worthwhile.

Rosinna

Sticks and Stones?

Every community has its bullies but when you live in Northern Ireland the type of bullying you get can be sectarian – it's all about your background, what religion you are, but it's really just an excuse for people to pick on each other.

I live in North Belfast and things can get pretty rough because there's a lot of Protestant areas and Catholic areas side by side. I remember one Sunday I went with my friends to Ballysillan Leisure Centre for a swim. Afterwards we were walking home and there was a group of girls standing outside the leisure centre. They said to us, 'Stay out of our area', but we just walked on past, not paying them much attention. Then, suddenly, six of them ran towards us. They were older than us, about 17 – we were about 15 – and one of them had a knife. 'Sing 'The Sash',[1] they said. Now, we didn't have a clue what

1 'The Sash' is a traditional 'Orange' (Loyalist) song that is offensive to Catholics. When members of the Orange Order parade, they often wear an orange sash.

'The Sash' was at that age, so we just stood there.

There was a man of about 40 coming towards us and we thought there was no way he'd just walk on past when he saw the girl pointing a knife at us. But all he did was mutter 'Fenian bastards'[2] and walk on. He wouldn't even come over and help. So we let on we were from Torrens, the Protestant estate, because we knew people from there and were able to name a few names. As they sort of knew the same people they let us go – they couldn't be sure we weren't Prods.[3] We walked away, really nervous, and when we got to the bottom of the street we started shouting up at them. It was just madness.

We were pretty used to that sort of thing though, especially since we moved to a secondary school that it was in a Protestant area. We used to have to walk home and we hated it every time. People would throw bricks at us and if we did get the bus the odd time, then they'd throw bricks at the bus instead. If we got the bus into town, we had to wait until later in the afternoon because otherwise all the girls from the local Protestant school would be on it. We travelled with them sometimes but it really wasn't worth it. They put chewing gum in our hair, spat at us, threw things at us. If we were unlucky we'd have to get the bus with them in the mornings too. They sat at the back and we had to sit at the front – it was like the blacks and the whites in Mississippi years ago. It was madness, but it's all calmed down now, because we're a bit older.

When I think about it all, it seems incredible that girls of my own age were doing this. And I know there was bound to be some nice girls on the bus as well – it's just that we never had a chance to meet outside, when we weren't in uniform. In a sense I know it was nothing personal – they didn't *know* us

2 Derogatory name for a Catholic.
3 Protestants.

– but the bullying still hurt. It was one extra thing I didn't need at that time.

Mind you, the boys were no better. One time we had to do some cross-community drama, so we went up to the boys' school to do a play with them. We had to hide in a cupboard during break times, to sit in a corner with a shovel in the door, because we got that much flak. It was the same at lunchtime – we couldn't move we were so scared. I remember one time when they got us on our way home. We went outside at about half past four to get a taxi. While we were standing at the school gates, waiting, we got bricks thrown at us. That taxi couldn't come quick enough!

It's not as bad now as it used to be, but you can still see the sectarianism. I was walking up past the Co-op shops only the other day and there was a girl there who had written 'All Taigs[4] are targets' and other sorts of things, graffiti, all over the wall. Outside our school it says 'All Taigs out' and 'All Taigs are bastards'. When we came back from our summer holidays one year, all the railings had been painted red, white and blue. And all the kerbies round the school, they're still red, white and blue.[5]

But it's the same on the other side. The kids in our street do start on the Protestants as well. And I suppose the Protestant kids just react to that – they want to get their own back. But, as I've said, it's not as bad as it used to be. It is getting better. I think there'll always be bullies around, but they won't be able to use the Troubles as an excuse for much longer.

---

4 Derogatory name for a Catholic.

5 Kerbies – kerb stones. Red white and blue are the colours of the Union Jack flag and denote a Loyalist political allegiance whereas green, white and gold are the colours of the flag of the Irish Republic.

Nanette

Different Strokes

I live in an exclusively Protestant area that got itself a 'bad name' during the Troubles. Some people think it must be a difficult place to live but I like it here and I wouldn't move away because everyone's so friendly – you just know everybody everywhere you go!

I'm the youngest of three sisters and one brother. My sisters all moved to different areas when they got married, but now they want to move back. I don't live with my mummy and daddy any more either, but my house is quite close to theirs.

Like everyone from my area, I went to a Protestant primary school and a Protestant secondary school. I think that might sound strange to someone who's not from here, but the schools aren't very mixed at all. Most of the state schools are Protestant and the Catholic schools are managed by the Catholic Church, (though the teachers aren't all nuns and priests!). Some Catholics do go to state schools, but it would be very rare for a Protestant to go to a Catholic school. There are also a few smaller integrated schools where Catholics and Protestants mix, but only a few people from my area go there.

So you see, in some places the two communities don't mix much at all – at least, not when you're young. The first Catholic girl I met was when we went away with our school to America for six weeks. I met this girl on the plane, and we stayed together for a day before we went to different families for the summer. I didn't see her in America, but we happened to be flying back together on our way home. We had a chat at the airport, but I didn't see her again after that even though we only lived about two miles away from each other.

I did come into contact with Catholics after I left school, but only because I took a job in a big shopping centre in a Catholic area. Me and my workmates were best of friends despite our different backgrounds; we went out everywhere together – nightclubs, house parties and so on. We always had a good laugh.

The only hassle I got was from some of the young fellas at the car wash outside the centre. They used to call me an 'Orange B******', said I 'shouldn't be over here' and should 'go back to where I came from'. They were the ones who would see me walking up from the Protestant estate. But our boys always used to watch where people walking into our neighbourhood came from too. It was just something that happened. Our boys thought they were protecting us, and their boys thought they were protecting their people. But at that level it was all bravado. I was never afraid, never felt in any kind of danger. The more I didn't react, or stood up to them, answering them back, the more they backed off. Like bullies everywhere.

I take an interest in some political things but I'm not really into it and I don't have a strong Unionist identity. My dad used to be in the Orange Order years ago, but not any more. I always used to say I was British, but my dad would say I was Northern Irish, or British Irish, or something else, not *just* British. I'm not as British as someone living in England and there's something of an Irish identity in me too. But I am more British than Irish. It's all so complicated! To be honest, it's hard to say what being British in Northern Ireland really means, but it's about being part of the UK and not part of the Republic of Ireland, I suppose. But saying that, I don't actually support the monarchy.

In terms of my background and culture, I suppose I am a Unionist and I do take part in the celebrations around the Twelfth. There's a good atmosphere, with the whole community coming together, putting up bunting, having a couple of drinks with friends, travelling around a couple of bonfires on the Eleventh night – around midnight the streets are full of people. Then there'd be more drinks, so that you usually get up on the Twelfth morning with a hangover. Then you'd go to see the main parade on the Lisburn Road.

For me the Twelfth isn't a political thing, it's just part of my culture. I think I have this view because religion doesn't really mean anything to me. I know that a lot of other people from the area feel differently. Some of them go on about how they hate Catholics and how they wouldn't let Catholics live here. Catholics have never done any harm to me, so I wouldn't mind if they lived in the same street.

The people who don't like Catholics tend to be men more than women – I really don't know why it's like that. I don't think I've ever met a boy round here who would actually say he likes Catholics but the girls don't seem that bothered.

I think the fathers pass their attitudes on to their sons and a lot of these boys will pass the same ideas on when they have children. I have a daughter at the moment, but I think if I had a son I would consider moving out of the area. I really wouldn't want him growing up with that attitude. I know that, no matter what I said, he'd pick it up on the streets. It's a vicious circle. No matter how hard you try to protect them or keep them out of trouble, they'd probably rebel against you anyway.

But for the moment I'm happy to stay where I am. It's where I grew up and my friends and family live here. There's such a good sense of community I think it will always feel like home.

Clare

Out on the Town

When I was in my teens, going out in Belfast was a lot different to the way it is now. Perhaps that's because I'm older, or perhaps it's because Belfast has developed into a much groovier place. Back then my social life consisted of going to our regular – a dark and dingy student bar. From the ripe old age of 15 we'd swagger up to the bouncers, armed with really bad false ID cards and with cigarettes hanging out of our mouths, desperately trying to look the legal age – most of us didn't, but being female seemed to help our cause! We did get turned away a few times, after the police had been in threatening to close the place down. Generally, however, underage drinkers were made most welcome – you were even given a little lollypop on the way in.

The first 'club' night I ever went to was Hellraiser, which was held in the Ulster Hall, a large city centre venue. It was aptly named I might add – from what I remember it really was what my mother would call a 'hellish den of iniquity' filled with what my friend Michelle would call 'complete and utter hallions'. I was nearly 16 and apart from being the first dance event I'd ever been to, it was also my first experience with drugs. Having no idea about the effects of any illegal substances, LSD seemed as good a thing to take as any. It didn't occur to any of us that it probably wasn't the best choice amidst a group of strangers who were busy 'E-ing' off their heads. Watching people with crazy bulging eyes and huge grins pass around Vics Vapo-Rub whilst you're tripping is not an experience I'm keen to repeat!

By the time I had finished my A levels I was really sick and tired of Belfast, so I went to university in Dublin. Like most students, the most important thing on my mind was checking out where to go out at night. Growing up in Belfast gives you little experience of other cultures and although Dublin might still be far behind cities like London and New York, it seemed incredibly cosmopolitan to me. We used to go to places where you could listen to good music and not get kicked out at one o clock.

Having said that, I returned to Belfast to complete my studies. It's my home and, for all its flaws, I love it. And, in a lot of ways, I think Belfast is a very exciting place to be right now. That may seem a strange thing to say about a city that's been blighted by troubles and seeped in disappointment, but if you've been out on a Saturday night to one of the new venues it has produced lately, places like Tatu and Milk, you might understand what I'm talking about. What makes the atmosphere even better is the sense that Belfast, a city that might once have been described as drab or even barren in terms of fun, is suddenly coming alive and that you're somehow part of it.

Most young people want more out of their night now than a few beers in Lavery's or the 'dance round your handbag' experience that you get from some of the old-style discos. That was all there was for a while, so to see a growth in clubs and bars which offer something different is great.

If I were to describe my usual Saturday night it would begin in a friend's house drinking a bottle of red wine. Sometimes I start off all pious and determined to have only a few but if it's been a crappy week then I look forward to getting really off my head – I know that may be a really stupid, irresponsible way to think but I also know I'm not alone. Drinking and to a lesser extent taking drugs is an integral part of what makes me and a lot of other people happy. It's part of our culture and while that's probably not a good thing, it's still good fun.

Lately, the people I hang around with will generally start off at Tatu. It's a bit of a 'beautiful people' place, but at the same time I get a kick out of being amidst this sort of crowd. It's like everyone is playing a game, so the clothes are nice and the music is good and the sofas are comfortable. It makes you feel good, if you allow yourself to get into it. It's not like the equally trendy Thompson's Garage, a bar and nightclub where I always get the impression that everyone is waiting for someone to explain the rules of the game.

I hope this doesn't make it all seem very pretentious – using words like 'groovy' and 'trendy' does make me a little nauseous! What I'm trying to say is that Belfast is a great spot because it hasn't been spoilt yet. There are more than a few posers, of course, but people are mostly down to earth and are just there to enjoy the ride. Belfast has been considered a backwater in terms of nightlife for so long, that I think it will take it a while yet before it becomes bored, cynical or pretentious.

I know it's probably sacrilegious to say so, but the reason I go to bars and clubs is to feed off the atmosphere rather than any genuine appreciation of the music. I'll be in a club like Milk or O'Neill's and someone will mention the name of a DJ and undoubtedly I'll adopt a very blank look. I do know that Belfast DJ David Holmes has hit the big time but I'm afraid that's about as far as my knowledge goes on that score.

Even though I have a great time going out here I do recognise that it isn't all a bed of roses. There's probably an ugly underbelly to most things and Belfast nightlife is no exception. Bouncers with God complexes; nasty, violent fights at three in the morning; date rape drugs – these things turn the carnival spirit sour. Again I think it's to do with getting the level right. I love clubbing but I have experienced nights where it all goes horribly wrong. Nights when someone you know gets beaten up, or you wake up scared and depressed and feeling like shit. But these things are not particular to Belfast; you have to think about safety everywhere. That said, you're only young once and I feel grateful to have enjoyed some of what my home town has to offer.

Katrina

The Best and Worst of Years

Last year I won a Millennium Award for my project in the community. My granny died too, so it was a hard year. After that, I went on a good long break to Australia. Now I'm back and raring to go.

The Millennium Award scheme is run by the Millennium Commission using money from the National Lottery. The scheme encourages young people to come up with project ideas to improve their own community. There were three Northern Ireland winners – two from upper Springfield and one from the Shankill[1] – and 24 altogether in the UK. My project was to make the community more aware of disabled people.

I was already working with a company that aimed to get disabled people out into the community. At the time, they

---

1 Springfield is a Nationalist area and Shankill a Unionist area of Belfast.

were only reaching out to mentally disabled people so when I joined I had to make them aware of the difference between mentally and physically disabled. I mean you can't mix the two; they are completely different. Cerebal palsy is my disability. I began to reach out to other young physically disabled people. It was very hard – I only managed to get a group of six young people together. One wanted help with getting a car, another wanted advice about getting a job. They didn't want to be in a group for physically disabled people just for the sake of it because they didn't want to be labelled. So we began to work on personal achievement programmes. The other thing we did was join in the company's Training For Life programme, which got us involved in all sorts of activities like canoeing. In fact, we were doing more than other able-bodied people our age!.

My birth mother is an alcoholic, so my grandmother looked after me from the moment I was born. My brother and sister also lived with us until I was about 13. Then they phoned our birth mother and ran away to be with her. When they ran away I had to contact Marie – that's my birth mother's name – and that contact damaged me a lot. When you see your brother and sister with your birth mother and there's a noticeable gap between you all, it's hard. I saw what it did to my granny. Anyway, that's why I call my granny Mummy. She had five grand-children living with her and two of her own kids. It was hard for her because she was a single parent but she had great faith.

Mummy began taking me to the healing waters in Lourdes, France, when I was about two – still a baby. She took me 17 times in total. Going to Lourdes 17 times, you don't really forget what it's like! It's a special place and even though I'm not that religious, I did enjoy going. The same three men would take a group of us three times a year, and I got on really well with one of them because I went so many times. People think you just go to mass when you go to Lourdes – you don't. You go round the grotto and you go to the baths. The first time I went, Mummy thought the nuns had killed me. They just threw me in and fished me out. She couldn't believe how rough they were. But it didn't result in a miracle cure. I was in a wheelchair until I was about 14.

I didn't always use the wheelchair – I didn't like using it in front of other kids because it made me different. So my mummy got patches and kneepads so that I could crawl about the street with the other kids. I must have gone through a pair of trousers a week! But she didn't care – she just wanted me to be free to move about. The neighbours would all go on at her saying, 'What are you doing, letting her go about like that?' But she didn't care, she wasn't going to wrap me up in cotton wool or make me stay in the house. She took me for what I was – always.

We did go through some bad times though. When I was about 14 or so, Mummy got an attack of arthritis. One morning she woke up and she couldn't move. No one else had ever taken care of me so my cousin from Africa, who lived in the same house and who was about three years older than me, started to look after me. But it wasn't the same.

Mummy's illness made me determined to try more and do more, and I really started pushing myself. You don't know how much you can do until that kind of thing happens. Sometimes I look back now and think, 'Well, that happened for a reason.' Mummy got better after a while and Katrina was a wee bit more independent!

The problem was that when she got better, Mummy expected to carry on as before. But I didn't need her as much now, and with me being more independent and rejecting some of her care, Mummy went through quite a lot of heartache. It was hard for her, especially when I started thinking about moving out two years later, when I was 16. I needed to see if I could survive on my own and I also wanted to let her see that I could do it so she wouldn't have to worry about me. I did try to move out, but by that stage we were the only ones left in the house, and I hated the thought of leaving her alone. I knew she would get lonely, and that because she was old, she wouldn't be around for much longer. She had given up her life to care for me, to care for all of us. So I stayed with her for the next four years, and last year she died of cancer. It was a hard time – we knew with her being an old woman that the end was going to come quick enough. So that's what happened. I wasn't meant to leave her – in the end she left me.

But my need for independence wasn't the only time I caused her heartache. One morning, when I was about 16, I woke up and hated my disability. It was all of a sudden – I can't explain it. I had never really noticed the way I was before, or I hadn't made a big deal of it, I suppose because I'd always been that way. But then I woke up and realised I was different. And I hated it. I wouldn't go anywhere. I stayed in the house. I told people I knew to go away when they phoned. I just wouldn't talk to anyone. When I eventually did go out I was afraid to open my mouth. I became very depressed.

I was at a special school and had been getting good grades. But when I went through this bad patch, I stopped working. What was the point in working? Whether you got an 'A' or a 'U', the teachers treated you as if you were great anyway, simply because you were disabled. I remember once when my brother Martin got a 'U', Mummy went absolutely haywire. Me, when I started doing badly, it didn't matter. I did good. I did bad. It didn't matter – the school always gave me a good report anyway. So I just gave up. I didn't bunk off school or anything, I just stopped working.

The teachers took the view that if they prepared us for the 'outside world' that was enough (I don't know where they thought we lived when we weren't at school!). And even then, the teachers' didn't have a clue. They told us that people in shops would tease us if we asked for help, so we should always take the money out of our purses ourselves. Well I can't do that. If I tried, it would take me about an hour to pay for something. I can't handle money – my hands don't work at that level. So what I do is open the purse and let people take the money out. Of course you get ignorant people who say, 'This isn't my job', but you deal with them. Most people understand and will count the money out themselves. But the teachers didn't approve of this. This said it was infringing on our 'autonomy'. I need to get by in life whatever way I can – what is the big deal about getting someone to get the money out of a purse for you?

And as for sex education...you must be joking! We were disabled people – we weren't meant to have sex. I really want a child, more than anything else. Last year I met a woman who was born able-bodied but developed a disability later on. I am now more able-bodied than she is. But she is planning to have a child with her partner. I would say that if I ended up with a disabled partner it would be hard to have a child, no matter how much I wanted one and I don't think I'd do it. There's a 99 per cent chance the child would be able-bodied but I see how my wee nephews and cousins get treated when their friends see me picking them up. They get teased about me.

I have gone out with able-bodied men, and my current partner is slightly disabled. When I was younger I wouldn't go with disabled people because it was like a bonus if you were with someone able-bodied. At the same time, though, I would always question why they were with me. I tried to be open about my disability – though I suppose it's fairly obvious anyway. A lot of able-bodied people take a long time to accept me. But then, it took me from the age of 14 until now (I'm 20) to feel comfortable with myself.

When my mummy saw what I was doing to myself, hating my disability, she got it hard. I'm just glad she saw me learn to drive. That was a big commitment. I had to get my own car, and there was a struggle with Disability Action, so Mobility paid for a car to be adapted. I got it last October, the month after we found out Mummy had cancer. I wanted her to see me drive, and she did see me taking lessons. On the morning of my test I got up to find that the house was packed – full of aunts, uncles, and cousins. My aunt came into my bedroom and said that Mummy was really sick. She said I wasn't to go into her room. 'Why?' I asked. 'Your granny's going to die today,' she said.

But I didn't believe her. The doctors in my life had always been wrong – saying I couldn't walk. But I was afraid anyway, crying and disturbed the whole day. At a quarter past six, my Australian aunty came in and said, 'Granny's away.' I went down into the room where she lay with my brother and my uncles all around her. I just looked at her. She had no hair. Chemo. I had to go outside and cry, just cry. I wouldn't wish it on my worse enemy. At least she got to know I was going to drive.

You never think that it will happen to you. What a year. In many ways the best, because I was working, and learning to drive, and getting the Millennium Award, but also the worst, because I lost my granny. That's why I had to take a holiday in Australia. I needed the break.

Carol

Too Close for Comfort

The city of Belfast is like a big patchwork quilt in terms of who lives where, particularly my area of North Belfast. If you had orange material for Protestant areas and green material for Catholic areas you'd have a big green bit in West Belfast, with an orange strip down the side, a big orange bit in East Belfast, and smaller green and orange bits in South Belfast. In North Belfast, you'd need individual strips for nearly every street. That's one of the first things you learn when you grow up in North Belfast – where you can go and where you can't.

Our estate is perched halfway up Black's Mountain, overlooking the rest of the city. There was a stage when we could walk through the neighbouring Protestant estate, Torrens, with no problems, but now there's too much tension. There are still some Protestants living in our street but they're all quite elderly. That's the mad thing – you can get on OK with Protestants living in your street but it changes when you go into an area that's exclusively Protestant. It's the same for Catholics too though; it cuts both ways. If a Protestant walked into the Ardoyne, they'd have big problems. It would depend on what area of the Ardoyne it was, of course, and what else was going on at the time.

A Protestant going into the Ardoyne on the 12 July, well that would be just madness. Our street is so close to Torrens, round the corner, and it's completely wild around the Twelfth. Every year the Protestants come into our street. There's no peace wall,[1] just some railings round the back and there's a load of deserted old houses the wee lads can come through to get on to our street. Other areas have peace walls to keep both sides separate, because it's too easy to attack each other. But we haven't got one. We phoned the Housing Executive and asked them to block up the houses but they wouldn't do it. And the police won't let us have a peace wall at the side of my house because they say it's not necessary. Try telling that to my stepdaddy. He was beaten up in his own home about four years ago, the year after the first Drumcree.[2]

It was Hallowe'en night. I heard shouting, so I looked out of my window and the next thing I saw was this man – I can still see it if I close my eyes – just lifting himself up over our garden wall. There was another man with him and the next

---

1 Peace walls were built between Protestant areas and Catholic areas in Belfast to try to prevent sectarian violence.

2 The Drumcree Orange parade has become a focus of growing civil unrest over the years. On one hand the march route goes up the Garvaghy Road, a Catholic area, so the residents object to the loyalists parading there. On the other, the loyalists say it is a traditional route and they have marched there for years. The Drumcree parade has resulted in rioting and a lot of political tension. Here, 'the first Drumcree' refers to the first year the Orange Order was banned from walking down the Garvaghy Road – the Orange order refused to acknowledge the ban and there was a stand-off with the police.

thing I knew, they'd started kicking our door in. I just froze. There was nothing I could do, it all happened so quick. They even closed the door behind them as they came in. They were that cheeky, they closed the door behind them. Everybody in the street was thinking, 'Oh God, there's something wrong', so the alarm was raised. But it was too late. They'd beaten my step-daddy unconscious.

The girl that lives next door to us was the first down at her door. When she came out she could see them jumping over the wall. The first one got away but she grabbed the second one by the leg and he turned round and he hit her. Her face was swollen up like a football.

There's not a year goes past that there isn't some kind of trouble. We get our windows put in with bricks all the time. Call the police? Don't make me laugh. There could be a full-scale riot on our street and no sign of the peelers. So then you get people standing guard outside your house for weeks, fellas our age, and some of them become really bitter. You can understand why.

Now, I just sleep through it all, but then I'd sleep through a bomb. If my mummy comes up and says the windows have been put in it doesn't scare me any more, I'm used to it. But my sister, our child, she'd be shaking like a leaf. There was one time the lads from Torrens put her bedroom window in and she wouldn't sleep there afterwards – she still won't unless my wee brother, who's 10 and thinks he's a real hard man, sleeps there too. She won't go up to the toilet by herself either. Even if she's in somebody else's house she still won't go upstairs by herself. You have to either stand at the bottom of the stairs or take her up. She was 2 when it started off. She's 6 now. She's been to counselling but it hasn't taken the fear from her. The counsellor's full of shit – she doesn't know what it's like living here.

I had top counselling – NOT! With Sister Siobhan, what a laugh. God love her, she didn't really know what she was on about. I went to her for about five years and she's still trying to get me to come back. But I just get on with it myself, me and my mates. We do just fine.

Jillian

Somebody Else's Conflict

I've just moved to England from Northern Ireland to go to college, but moving is nothing new in my family. My grandfather's family moved from where they originated in Lithuania – a lot of my family are from Lithuania – when the hatred broke there. So my family has experienced plenty of anti-Semitism in our time and that's one reason why we don't get involved here – it's somebody else's conflict.

My mum and dad met up here, when the community was bigger than it is now. It used to be about a thousand strong but now it's only about 100 people, and about 70 per cent of them are over 70 years of age. The decline is connected to the Troubles. When the community saw that there was going to be trouble, they started moving again – not because they were targeted, but because the environment was troublesome. I think this could be because of the tradition of continuous exile, of always moving on. If it hadn't been for the Troubles I think there would be a lot more Jewish people here today.

My dad is a dentist and worked on the Shankill Road, which he loved. He learnt a lot from mixing with the people there and he really enjoyed the crack.[1] Before that he worked in Lisburn, about 10 miles outside Belfast. Then in 1993, the Shankill bombing[2] happened. He wasn't at work that day because it was a Friday – he always takes Fridays off as part of the Sabbath – but his surgery was directly opposite the fish shop where the bomb went off. It was severely damaged, windows shattered, and all the TV crews took their footage from his office. The bombing put things in perspective for him – he decided he wanted to move away from the Shankill, and moved back to working in Lisburn.

Because the Jewish community is so small, it's not promoted the way it is in England. We do have a synagogue, but there's only one religious instructor, and he's not a fully qualified Rabbi. To be honest I've been starved of real Jewish life growing up in Northern Ireland. Any contact I had was with Jewish youth groups in England. When I was 16 I went to Israel – it was fantastic to have that opportunity, but when I came back, even though life was great, I missed the Jewish element I'd experienced in Israel.

Speaking Yiddish or German was one of the few ways I could identify with my traditions. My grandparents speak Yiddish and I picked up quite a lot from them. I also learnt German and we sometimes speak German or Yiddish in the house. When I'm out with my family and there's something I want to say, sometimes it'll come out English sometimes German, sometimes Yiddish. It just depends.

---

1 Fun, jokes, or a good time.
2 Ten people were killed by an IRA bomb at a fish shop on the Shankill Road, Belfast.

In other ways, I've experienced a lot of cultural diversity in Northern Ireland. I mean, I was Jewish, and my two best friends were a Catholic and a Protestant! What more could you ask for? My parents always wanted as much racial diversity as possible in my environment. I was never sent to a Protestant or Catholic, but an integrated school – on the very premise that I would mix with other races and creeds. At primary school we were taught that everyone was equal. That was the theory anyway, but the reality can be quite different, as I discovered when I went to secondary school.

I wasn't really affected by other people's prejudices until I was in form three. Then when I was about 13 or 14, I was bullied and towards the end, they started bringing my religion into it. They would say things like 'Heil Hitler' and 'All Jews should die.' The bullying had been going on for a while with all sorts of taunts, but I could handle those. It was only when they started using religion that it really got to me; I realised I had to do something about it. I wouldn't even say they targeted me *because* I was Jewish; it was just another piece of ammunition they could throw, and it was one that hurt. The thing about the school was that there were Hindus, Christians, Muslims, Chinese, Koreans – you name it, they'd all been there and I'd seen them experience hatred. But until then I'd never been on the receiving end. To look at me you wouldn't know I'm Jewish – but the others were obviously different in Northern Ireland because of their dress or skin colour.

Normally the school came down on any racial harassment like a ton of bricks. But I found that they didn't really know how to handle my problem. Instead of punishing the girls who were teasing me, they spent more time checking to see if I was OK and I don't think that worked – they should have come down harder on the bullies. I was doing my Duke of

Edinburgh at the time and they kept on at me. I will never ever forget that, the Heil Hitler taunts. They will stay in my memory as long as I live. It made me realise what it must be like for people who experience racism every day of their lives – something you don't fully understand until you become a victim yourself.

When I started going out, there was never any real issue about my religion, but I was always told not to broadcast it. One of the problems I did find was that my parents often wouldn't let me go out because of the Troubles. If I wanted to go into town it was always, 'Oh you never know what paramilitary group might try to bomb that club', or, 'There might be trouble there you know.' Gradually as I got older my parents gave me more freedom, but even last year, when I was 17, and I wanted to go downtown, they asked me not to go because there'd been some problems.

Living here you do see what happens when two religious groups clash, and you think, 'Is it worth it?' A lot of people in England generally don't understand the whole Northern Irish thing, asking is it not like living in a war zone – it's just what they see on the TV, I suppose. But it's not like that. My 18 years in Northern Ireland have been the best of my life.

I suppose in moving to England, I'm keeping up the tradition of moving on. People are leaving the community in Dublin now too – there's only about 2000 Jews left there. There are just so many more Jews in England – it's a huge community, especially in North-West London – thousands upon thousands. The downside is that there is also lot of anti-Semitism. Apart from the bullying at school, I didn't really experience any serious anti-Semitism in Northern Ireland. When I tell my Jewish friends in England this they can't believe it because it's always been a part of their lives. While I haven't experienced it yet myself, I've certainly seen it: in pictures, in graffiti, and on murals.

So, now that I'm in England, I'm mixing with a lot more Jewish people, especially as I'm staying in a Jewish hall of residence at college. The other week, one of the guys in my residence asked me where I was from and I said Northern Ireland. First of all he said, 'Whereabouts in Scotland is that?' And then he proceeded to ask me – himself a Jew living in the Jewish halls of residence – whether I was a Catholic or a Protestant!

Emma

Jumping the Hurdles

As a child I had dyslexia but it wasn't discovered until I moved to a new primary school. I was having a lot of trouble at my first school. Although my reading was very good, I kept writing in block capitals, and my work was suffering. My mum was young when she had me, only 16, so she didn't have the confidence to approach the school about the problems I was having. Moving schools gave me a chance – they picked up the condition and I got support.

My mum was never married to my dad – they'd fallen out while my mum was pregnant and then she got married to someone else. She met my stepfather when I was about three, and had two other children with him. At first it was OK but then when I was six or seven they decided to tell me my stepfather wasn't my real dad and they didn't handle it very well. All it did was open up a whole load of new questions for me – was she really my mummy and were these really my brother and sister? Then there was my stepfather's alcoholism, which he's only getting help for now.

My mum was quite ill when I was younger; she was agoraphobic. It all started when she was about 15 – she started getting panic attacks whenever she was travelling. Looking back she says it wasn't very serious but she mentioned it to the doctor and he put her on valium, and she became addicted to it. Even when she was able to come off the valium the agoraphobia stayed. She's been a lot better recently and has started university and travels a bit. But when I was younger, it was still bad and because I was the oldest I had to care for the younger children, taking them to school because she couldn't leave the house. It all made me feel older than I actually was.

When I was in my early teens, things at home started to break down even further and I rebelled. At the time I blamed my stepfather, and his drinking, but looking back it was very much a family thing – Mummy had had a nervous breakdown in the past and there were a lot of issues that had never been sorted out. It all came to a head when I was 13 or 14.

By this stage I had a boyfriend. He was four years older than me and came from a very bad family background. But that didn't matter – he was a rock to cling to because things were so bad at home. I could spend all my time with him. Other friends couldn't just be out all day, they had to go home for their dinner, whereas nobody really cared where he was. I didn't want to be at home with my family, and they probably didn't want me there either, so he was my escape.

It was my boyfriend who told me about the care system. Lots of his relatives had been in care, although he hadn't been himself. I'd got to the stage where I just couldn't stand being at home for one moment longer so I decided I wanted to go into care. It was all my own idea. I'd never had any contact with the care system before – we'd never had a social worker involved in the family because there were never issues of neglect or anything. We'd always been well looked after. But living with them was just doing my head in.

I arrived at the social services office and said 'I want to go into care'. The duty social worker came in. She was quite a young girl, from somewhere in the south of Ireland. I spent the whole day with her while she rang around. The office rang my mummy, who cried and said to send me home, but my mind was made up. I said, 'No way, I'm not going home, I'm not going to live there anymore.' The social worker said, 'Look, there is no place for you.' I was only 14 but I said, 'Well, get me a duvet and a pillow 'cos I'm not going home. This is it.'

Eventually they admitted me. I remember arriving at this huge building with big gates and a wall outside it. I had no idea what the place was for or what to expect. 'But this is a convent, there're nuns here,' I said when I clapped eyes on it. I didn't know that it was a children's home. 'Am I meant to stay here?' I was in for a big shock.

The first night I arrived I hadn't eaten all day – it was about 8.30 pm – and they gave me the keys and told me to go to the store. I thought, 'Right, OK. I can do this.' I arrived down at the storeroom and everything was in bulk – big freezer bags of this and that. I had no idea how to cook – I didn't even know how to turn the big industrial cookers on. I panicked. 'Oh my god. What have I done? What am I gonna do? How am I going to look after myself? These people aren't going to look after me.'

What I hadn't realised was that the 'children's home' was actually an adolescent unit and they were expecting me to be able to do these basic things for myself. Then it hit me that maybe things at home hadn't been as bad as I thought. As I talked to the other people there I realised that some of them had been having a much worse time than me. I had had so much freedom at home; I was treated as an adult as long as I didn't bother anybody. My dinner was made but I didn't have to be home any particular time to eat it – I could heat it up in the microwave. As long as I came home at some stage during the night my family didn't really mind.

In the unit there were rules like 'You must be back for dinner' and 'You can only go out if you're going to a friend's house and their parents agree that you're going to be there.' I found myself getting into trouble because my boyfriend was still around, and I was staying out late with him. Now that I work with young people in residential care, I know that not all children's homes are like that. The one I happened to be in was very rigid and I found it hard going.

But half of it was great because even though there were various things wrong with the unit, there was no personal stuff. For me it was an escape from family issues; it meant not having to deal with them. Mummy would come round nearly every day and she liked that – it was an escape for her too. I could, and still did see my brother and sister and my grandparents.

So, for me, life carried on, but in a better way. I had space away from the family and the only drawback was all the rules and regulations. I ended up staying there about eight months. Then I went one step too far. Because I was there on a voluntary order, they could throw me out any time and that's exactly what they did when I started staying out at night. They said I should go to Rathgael, which was a much stricter training school about ten miles from home, but there wasn't a place, so I had no choice. I moved back in with the family, only to find that the circumstances I had left behind were still there.

This time I could only stick it for a couple of months. I really did try to hold it together because I was only 15, still too young to move out on my own. During my time at the children's home I'd been assigned a social worker but I very rarely saw her, only once a month or so. The social workers at the home didn't really look at any of the family stuff, or talk about it. They never tried to resolve the problems and only discussed day-to-day issues like school.

When I moved back home I started attending an Adolescent Support Unit that a guy called Harry ran. Like the last place I'd been in, this was state-run, but you got real therapy this time. It's shut down now. I stayed there in respite care[1] for up to ten days at a time and then went back home. But it was getting to the stage where even respite care was not going to work.

Then came the opportunity to get a flat with Barnardos Leaving Care programme. I thought they'd never give me a flat, but Harry's team, the social workers and Barnardos all worked closely together to say that I was more mature than 15 and would be able to look after myself.

It was fantastic – just the break I needed – and it was close enough to my family that I could visit them, but on my own terms. The programme was great – they called out to see me and gave me support. I was in fourth year at school and as I was too young to get the brew,[2] social services paid my rent and gave me a living allowance of about £30 a week.

It was also really strange. Already I felt a bit older than some of my schoolmates and when people at school were talking about having a bottle of cider in the park, I was thinking I had

---

1 Respite care gives the person short breaks away from living with the family.
2 Unemployment benefit/Jobseekers Allowance.

to toe the line because I don't want to get thrown out of my flat by Barnardos. They'd been very good to me and I couldn't – and didn't want – to go home. My relationship with the rest of my family was improving *because* I wasn't there any more, and me and my mum were beginning to sort things out. I had blamed her for a lot of things, but in some ways she had been a great parent. Of course, in other ways she hadn't but it wasn't until I moved out that I began to appreciate her situation. I couldn't see how young she'd been when she'd had me. She'd had a lot to cope with, her illness and all the family problems, as well as trying to do a good parenting job. At the time all I could feel was, 'You were supposed to be my parent, why weren't you?' I'm now able to accept that it's hard in the real world. If all my mum and I could expect to have was being like sisters, then that was enough. (It's only now that we can talk very openly about this.)

School was a problem, though, because I didn't want to get up in the mornings, I didn't want to wear a uniform, I didn't want to act like I was 15 when I was living in my own flat and looking after myself. Barnardos were very supportive and understanding. I think I still connected school with all the problems I'd had because of my dyslexia and at one point my absenteeism got so bad that I had to go to court. Then I found out I was pregnant.

I had just turned 16 a few months ago; a wee bit older than my mummy had been when she had me. I was still with the same boyfriend, the one who'd told me about the care system, but by the time the baby was born he was no longer on the scene. He went to England. Let's just say he was asked to leave by people in the community and I wasn't going to go off with someone I knew I couldn't trust and end up god knows where. I was much too sensible. He was begging me to go with him, and I adored him, but I thought, I'm pregnant, I can't land in England with nowhere to live. I knew my priorities; I was thinking about cots and prams, not floating around England. It was a difficult decision but one that had to be made. And I knew that he wouldn't have stuck around very long anyway. It wouldn't have worked.

I turned 17 and became a single mother all in the space of a few weeks. When Ruth was born the labour was awful. I had no idea how painful it was going to be. People lie; they tell you dreadful lies about how it's not as bad as you think. It's worse. But there's no point in thinking about it because you just have to do it.

Ruth weighed 9lb 14 oz when she was born, such a big baby and so alert. I remember in the hospital when she was about two days old, I went off down the corridor to have a bath. The nurse came up to me and said, 'I think your baby's crying.' And it took me a second to realise, 'She's talking to me. *My* baby's crying. And they expect me to get out of this bath and go and look after her? My god, I've just given birth and I have to cope.'

The other thing I noticed in hospital was that they treated me differently to the other mothers. When they called my name it was Emma Coates, while everyone else was Mrs So and So. I felt unable to ask any questions, because I was so young, and felt really ashamed of being alone and pregnant. When I got out of hospital, I thought that, as a young single mother, people were judging me. If Ruth cried in public I'd feel uncomfortable, thinking that everyone would think I couldn't take care of her. I wanted to tell them, 'I can! I can look after her, look, she's lovely and clean.' I always felt I had to prove myself.

It was hard being on my own all the time. Mummy was

shocked and upset at first – I think she wanted to be supportive but found it very difficult. She did come round in the end and then she was brilliant. I found I had a new respect for everything she'd been through. At the same time, I didn't want to do things the way she'd done them. I knew that even though mummy had no qualifications she was very intelligent and that if she hadn't had me she could have gone on with school (in fact she's now doing a degree). I also knew that I had ability too because even though I'd not done much work at school, I still seemed to pass exams. I had been raised with the feeling that I could do something else, that there was more to life.

So I took maternity leave for about a year. I was working part-time in a chippy at night and working in a coffee shop on Saturdays. Then I went and did a GCSE. I think I wanted to prove I could do something. I did the exam part-time and only got a D grade, but knew it was because I'd been moving (to a Housing Executive house near my mum) and I hadn't put the work in. I knew I wasn't stupid.

I also became involved in a research project on young mothers. While I was pregnant, the Save the Children Fund had approached me through Barnardos and asked me if I was interested. When they first asked me I knew nothing about being a young mother – being pregnant doesn't mean you automatically understand the reality of it all. They were offering travelling expenses and childminding so I thought this is something to do. It's a way to meet other people and it's a bit of extra money. Great! I was interested in the issues but I didn't think it would turn into much more than that.

The first year of Ruth's life wasn't all plain sailing, though. I probably had some post-natal depression during this time and didn't even realise it. I was physically there, but not emotionally. Sometimes the days passed in a blur. Even looking back now at photos I don't remember her being that small.

But the project did help me with my confidence. It got me in touch with a support worker, Lorna, and started me thinking I had something relevant to say. Then, towards the end of the project, a job at VOYPIC (the Voice of Young People in Care) came up. I'd been to a couple of meetings on young people with experience of the care system and I'd been interested in the issue for a while, though it was difficult to attend meetings with Ruth. The job was for someone aged between 18 and 25 and the salary was £11,500 – more money than I'd ever dreamed of. 'There's no way I could get this,' I thought. But the team encouraged me to go for it so I thought, 'What have I got to lose?' I got it and I was absolutely amazed. It's made the biggest difference to me.

I'm a Development Work Mentor now. I do loads of really diverse things – everything from being here on a Sunday with young volunteers, attending a report launch in the Department, and afternoon workshops on young people in care and education. I'm the only young person who's here as a paid worker.

The other thing about the job is that VOYPIC supported me back into education – they paid for it and gave me time out for classes. Others went back and did grand things. I went back and did GCSEs and got an 'A' grade in English. To be dyslexic and be able to get the top grade in English was like getting a degree to me! Now I'm halfway through the first year of the Community Youth Work course at the University of Ulster and I'm really enjoying it. I had to go through an interview process and again there was that thing: 'Will I get on? I have no academic background.' It all seemed like a big hurdle to overcome.

I think my dyslexia made me think that people would see me as stupid. I don't have severe dyslexia; it's mild, but the stigma is still there. When I got on the course I thought they were all going to find out. I was frantic about the first essay and had everyone helping me. I've done my fourth one now, I've got my grades back, and I'm doing well. Next year I'm doing a placement in Rockford, Illinois, for eight weeks and taking Ruth with me. She's 4 now.

I did have the attitude of 'I'm not going to make the same mistakes as my mum' – getting pregnant young. But I did. I also realise, though, that the circumstances are very different. Having a job has meant I don't feel trapped at home like my mum did. I spent the first year of Ruth's life only leaving her to go to part-time work. I was with her all day and night, whereas now she's at school and I'm working so when I get to see her I spend valuable time with her. Last night we went to the panto, something we both enjoy. We make time. When I was at home all day I wasn't making time, I was just doing it, just coping, not even enjoying it. Some people put on a show and say looking after a baby is the most wonderful thing but I don't remember it like that; I remember it being really hard. It was more like a duty than a pleasure and a lot of people feel that way. But you don't admit it, you say, 'Its great.' Well it's not. It's hard. Once I started going out to work, I realised I did miss Ruth a great deal and I looked forward to the weekend and the evenings so that I could spend time with her. It was getting the balance right that mattered.

Now I feel so much more confidence thanks to the job and an education – that confidence carries over into dealing with Ruth's school, with doctors, realising that I know best, having confidence in myself as a parent. The difference in the relationship between her and me, and me and my mum is that

I want to be the mother, I never want to be the big sister. I'd like her to be able to confide in me, as her mother. She's so much fun; I really enjoy her company. There's nothing I like better than to have a night in and have a laugh with her. I really wouldn't be without her for the world.

Sinead

Out and About

She said to me, 'I'll walk you home.' And I thought 'She's been to university; she's been out in the big wide world.' So I said to her, 'Have you ever thought about kissing a girl?' She was a bit taken aback. 'Oh!' There was a sharp intake of breath. 'Whaddya mean, who've you been talking to?' I knew I'd hit a raw nerve – my 'gaydar' was already well developed!

So she walked me up to my house. Then I walked her back down to get a taxi. Then she walked me back up to my house again. I had school the next morning and here I was, faffing around in the middle of the night. My mother was going to kill me. And I had an English essay to do, so my teacher was going to kill me too.

As we walked back up the street again, we just stopped suddenly, facing each other, chatting about nothing. And I said 'Would you mind if I kissed you?' She said, 'No.' And I just knew when I kissed her that this was the business; this was what had been missing all along.

I'd been out with a few boys, but it never really did anything for me – I could never connect with them on a deeper level. For a while I thought, 'Oh, I'm just not getting the right bloke.' I was used to fighting with boys at school when I was younger, playing football with them, hanging out with them. But I was never into holding their hands or getting involved in a serious way.

I ended up going out with this woman, Jenny, the first woman I ever kissed, for three and a half years. And nobody ever knew. I'm sure they had their suspicions, but they didn't voice them. In all that time the only other person I told was a close friend I knew I could trust. It took me a while, though – I didn't say anything until about two years into the relationship. My friend was fine about it – she even said she could have told me already! And true to her word, she never said a thing about Jenny to anyone. She went to America for a while and when she returned the gossip was out; everyone was saying, 'Oh, did you hear the crack,[1] Sinead's a lesbian.' She just replied that she'd known for years!

So Jenny was my first girlfriend, and she was an older woman. But it was to be a very frustrating relationship because Jenny wasn't very 'out'. At all. When we went out on the town, it was always just as 'friends'. No meaningful glances, secret smiles or flirting in public – she was so careful about that. It was the first time in my life I felt I could love another person in that way, yet I wasn't allowed to let my feelings show. But I was very much in love with her, so I put up with it.

Because Jenny and I couldn't act like a couple in public, and

1 Crack – pronounced crack. An absolutely brilliant time (it was a good crack), someone who is great fun (they're a good crack) or the latest piece of gossip (have you heard the crack?).

she wasn't about to hit the gay nightspots, we used to spend hours driving around in her car, hoping nobody would see us. We turned into experts on the local flora and fauna seeing as we visited all the local beauty spots with amazing regularity. Parked out in the middle of nowhere, who would see? Who would suspect we weren't just admiring the view? We weren't even having sex; it was just good to be with each other, to be able to hold somebody's hand. Yet I felt like Jack the Ripper, sneaking around in dark alleyways and lay-bys. We weren't doing anything wrong: all I was doing was loving somebody, and all she was doing was loving me back. Yet we always had to keep it quiet.

And there was the added surprise of the soldiers – you just never knew where they were going to pop up! One night we'd parked on this small country road and we were kissing. The next thing there was a knock on the window. I turned round and went 'Shite!' I didn't have my glasses on so I couldn't see properly, but there was this soldier leering through the window and he was all blacked up – all you could see were the whites of his eyes and his teeth! Jenny was panicking (I think she could see the news headlines!), but I wound down the window, and tried to look in control. The soldier said, 'All right there'... he paused as he looked from me to Jenny, then added with a grin, 'ladies'? Next thing he had called over two of his mates, and they were asking us, 'What were you two up to? We didn't think any of that went on over here!'

The soldiers wanted to know our names and Jenny started to get very stressed, because we were in her dad's car and she didn't want him to find out about us. The soldiers really put us through it – Is this car stolen? No it's not, it's just hot – they even radioed through the registration number to check we weren't lying. Then they started to take the piss – they got us out of the car and asked us what height we were, what colour were our eyes. They knew we were going to give them whatever information they wanted, just so that we could get away. When they learned that I was 18 and Jenny was 22 they called her a cradle snatcher.

I was so relieved when they finally let us go.

Like most relationships, my one with Jenny had its ups and downs. The real downside of keeping it quiet came when we had a row. All the other girls in school could support each other when they were going through boyfriend trauma because they'd all had the same experience, they'd been through the same thing at one stage or another. Whereas I could only say my problem was a 'friendship' issue, which meant it wasn't treated as seriously.

On top of all that Jenny used to do things to 'allay suspicion'. Like going out with boys in front of me. We used to go to a place called the Pink Pussycat (and no, I haven't made that up) on Friday nights and she'd quite often hook up with some guy there. She seemed to think it was OK to go out with other people but I was too much in love with her to go off with someone just for the sake of getting back at her. I remember watching her slow dance with a guy right in front of me and it just broke my heart. And I couldn't even tell people what was wrong with me.

When I left school Jenny had moved to Belfast, and I used to go and visit her from Wednesday through to Sunday. Then, after a while, she started making excuses, saying she wouldn't be around and could I come up on Friday or Saturday instead. I found out she'd started going steady with a bloke.

Jenny hates being gay, even now. I still see her sometimes and she is so angry; she just hasn't come to terms with it at all. I realise that she directed a lot of that anger at me, almost as if she held me responsible, but I just didn't see it properly at the time because it was what I expected out of a lesbian relationship – I had nothing else to measure it by. And, of course, I also had that 'it's wrong to be gay, God says it's wrong, you're wrong' thing going on in my head. So I was confused. It made me think that perhaps only a heterosexual relationship offered a chance of being happy. I went through a time when I felt extremely angry about the whole situation and the way Jenny had treated me, and it's only now, in my early twenties, that I'm starting to get rid of those feelings.

I didn't come out to my mum until I was 21. I'd been unofficially out at college for a while – going to gay clubs and that – but it came to me as I was due to get on a plane one day: if I die on this flight, it's going to be a very colourful funeral. Adam and Adam and Eve and Eve will be there. The drag queens will be bitching over nail varnish in the church. I realised I *had* to tell my mother because if something did happen to me she'd not only have to cope with me being dead, but also with me being gay! So there I was standing at the kitchen sink and I just said to her 'I have something to tell you. I'm gay.' She laughed weakly and looked at the TV which wasn't on – I don't know why, some form of reality check maybe? Then she turned her head to look at me and said, 'Huh! Tell me something I don't know.' I'd been shitting myself about this, and she already knew!

'Yeah, well you're as well rid of thon one,' she continued. She meant Jenny.

'So you don't mind?' I said.

I can still remember her reply so, so clearly: 'Sinead, lesbian, straight, whatever, as long as it makes you happy. It's what you are, and it's not going to make you any different in my eyes.'

Jayne

A Local Girl at Heart

I'd always been interested in politics, but what people here would call politics with a small 'p'. I was involved in debating at school, but that was mostly about things like what should be sold in the school tuck shop, nothing serious. In Northern Ireland 'Politics' with a capital P is what we used to describe debates on whether Northern Ireland should be part of the United Kingdom, or whether it should join with the Republic of Ireland to form a United Ireland. It's a pity that the bread and butter issues that were important for ordinary people, like health and education, didn't get the airtime that they should have. Somehow our news was always dominated by 'The Constitutional Question'. Health and education mustn't have been exciting enough.

For me, the real politics lay in the countryside where I lived. Mine was a farming family and from the age of about 15, I did a lot of my father's administrative and research work. Word got around, so people would come and ask me for help when they had any problems, in getting funding, for example, or advice on who to contact at the Department of Agriculture. Through this, I developed a lot of knowledge about a broad range of issues.

My family was also a Unionist family and my father was a member of the Ulster Unionist Party. I got involved in the party in a very low-key way at university and then joined my local branch association. The contacts and networks I could tap into through the party were also useful for my advice work. So, even though I was steeped in Unionist culture – I was British, I attended Orange marches, I was Protestant – there were practical reasons for wanting to join. I wanted to be in the party not just for cultural reasons, but for economic reasons too.

I did have some reservations. The UUP, like every political party in this country, is not perfect. We've focused on the constitutional question – the 'them' and 'us' – at the expense of other issues. For 30 years we've never actually sat down and thought about what our core values might be. If you look across the parties, there are people within the SDLP and the UUP who share a common attitude to say, socialism, or capitalism. When joining, I thought, 'Well, OK, I might not agree with every policy within the UUP, but in general it reflects a great deal of my identity.'

I feel that I'm British, and identify with British history and culture. But I'm also a local girl at heart and you'll find that with a lot of Unionists. They want to remain part of the Union, but they also have a strong Northern Irish identity. How can someone living in London really know and gauge the opinion of someone in Northern Ireland? It's different here – as different as Scotland is from England. Our identities are different. So even though we are British there is a strong sense of local autonomy – Unionists want Northern Irish people to be able to govern ourselves. We identify with the Union, but also with here. We want to be able to control our farming, and other central issues. For 30 years we were governed directly from London – Direct Rule it was called. And, as much as some people might have enjoyed that system, having our own devolved government, and a fair one at that, is much better. You can get sidelined at Westminster. One half of our people hate the British government, one half hates the Irish government, so if we are administrating our own affairs, we can just get on with it!

Joining the party has supported that identity and it has proved to be a real experience. When I started to talk at meetings that threw a few of them. 'It's a woman. She can talk!' Actually, when I debate with them, nine times out of ten I win. Probably because I shout the loudest. But at our branch level women are quite well represented – there is a woman Chair and women Office Bearers. Yet somehow, when it comes to going for election, they just won't, they don't want to put themselves up as candidates. And it's not just them, it's a reflection of the mindset across the province. I think each political party is finding it difficult to sell women candidates. The idea that women are 'still in the kitchen' exists, and it's not helped by various people who actually tell women to 'get back to the kitchen'. We have as much to offer as men, sometimes maybe more. We can see the psychological impact of decisions on ordinary people; we are still the main ones raising children; we have a central role in society. Political parties haven't tapped into that yet.

From this slightly shaky start I came up through the ranks and now I'm a delegate to the Ulster Unionist Council at branch level in the country, even though I now live just outside Belfast. I realised that if I was going to make a difference, it would be by being on the Council. It wasn't planned, but I'm glad that I'm on it, because I now have direct input.

I suppose then that I am something of a rarity in the UUP. I am a young person and a woman. You do get treated slightly differently. I now have a job for the party, working for one of the Members of the new Assembly as his political researcher and adviser. When I first started a couple of people thought that I was a secretary. Not that there's anything wrong with being a secretary – it's just the assumption that annoys me. Would they say the same thing about a young man? After a while they realised I could do all the other things – I could work at branch level, I could speak, I could do the marketing, I could do the administration. I wasn't an expert at everything, but I was a competent all-rounder. It's only now after two years of working at their level that elected Assembly Members will come up and ask my advice. I'm not complaining about taking two years to get this far, part of it is my age as well, I think. They look at me and think 'she probably wouldn't know, she doesn't have too much experience.

But I know that I have built up that experience and if I was given the chance, I would stand for election. For me preparation is everything. I want to build myself up so that when I do run I will have a fair chance. I don't want to end up saying, 'I didn't get this seat because I wasn't prepared.' I want to be trained and professional. You need to build yourself up by working within the party and making contacts in the local area. Get yourself a good name. Do the work, get the credit. And run to win.

Anna

University Challenge

When I first started at Queen's I was very apprehensive; I didn't really like Belfast at all. I was from the country, and didn't want to stay in the city. Even though I had the grades to get into university, I had no confidence in myself and wondered all the time, 'What am I doing a degree for? I haven't a clue.' I was going to jack it in, but I knew that would mean I'd have to get a job, be responsible, and maybe even grow up a little more. The easier option was to stay at university and that's what I did.

I'd go home every weekend to see my boyfriend – I was completely besotted with him. My home town was about 25 miles away and he would come to see me every Wednesday during the day, then pick me up on a Friday for the weekend. I never really got involved in student life – I didn't use the Students' Union at all, only went out one night a week, got blitzed on a Thursday and went home on a Friday. All that was to change . . .

University was a time for finding my own feet politically because coming from my background – a rural Catholic, and thus, theoretically, a Nationalist – I did have a problem with my identity. It was a case of, 'Am I Irish? or, 'Am I Northern Irish?' I was doing a politics degree so I knew that this sort of question was going to come up all the time.

I'd always had a social conscience, and supported the welfare state. I believed in equality between men and women, and I knew that education should be a right for all, not a privilege for those who can afford it. I did not believe that by some accident of birth, the monarchy and the upper classes had the right to live off the backs of the people – Republicanism in the broadest sense of the word. I also believed that the people best equipped to govern Ireland lived on the island itself. So I felt my identity emerging as Irish and Republican.

I said I didn't get into the Students' Union in my first year. But I certainly made up for it in my second and third years! I joined the politics society and thought 'What a bunch of complete and utter tossers.' But then I met people who inspired me – one guy told me about the history of Queen's Students' Union and how, from the 1960s, it had been a hotbed of both political thinking and action. In fact, the Civil Rights Movement had sprung from political meetings held there.

So before I knew it I was elected for student council. When you are involved in the council *and* you're studying politics you can be subjected to some of the most bigoted things you'll ever hear in your life. The problem is, these sorts of comments put your back up and you immediately become defensive. That means it all turns into a war of words where nobody really listens to anyone's point of view. It just entrenches your own beliefs because you're busy thinking, 'They're nothing but a bunch of right-wing fascists.'

And of course I didn't think I was narrow-minded because I was a socialist and a Republican: everybody had the right to be what they wanted to be. You know the old chestnut- 'I may not agree with what you say but I'll fight to the death for your right to say it'. But the reality was that people weren't able to be what they wanted to be, or say what they felt. It really used to enrage me when somebody who claimed they were open-minded said we couldn't have a Lesbian, Gay and Bisexual Rights Officer in the students' union because being lesbian or gay was perverted. Or that there was no need for a Women's Rights Officer because women should be at home barefoot, pregnant, and chained to the cooker. Or that the Cultural Affairs Officer's job was not to promote and represent the diverse cultures that made up the student body at Queen's, but to promote only Irish culture in order to intimidate, and disenfranchise Protestant students and keep them out of the Student Union, which was, after all, a 'Republican stronghold'. The sad fact is now that I'm working, I still come across people like this.

Thankfully not everyone was as opinionated. It was in my second year that I met the daughter of a woman I'd always greatly admired who had been involved in the Civil Rights Movement of the 1960s. Like me, the daughter was involved in student politics and we became great mates. The union building became our home and we had good crack[1] there.

It was also around this time that I went to my first women's meeting. The Women's Rights Officer for that year hadn't been elected to the Students' Union Executive yet. The Deputy President had put posters up all over the union saying, 'Come Along To The Women's Meeting: Free Beer!', so me and two mates decided to go along. After all, there was free beer.

---

1 Fun.

One of my mates was such an ardent feminist she could establish a feminist critique on the basis of the information on a cornflake packet – scary! The Deputy President was a woman I knew from school and she frightened the life out of me as well. The other woman hosting the meeting was the Welfare Officer – she was a strange skinny creature with dyed red hair and a London accent, wearing stripy tights underneath a miniskirt, and dragging for dear life on a fag. I thought that she was a real weirdo. So the women's group was somehow established that year from drinking McEwan's lager – there were crates of the stuff and only six of us. It was a long night.

One of the issues that really interested me was the under-representation of women in politics in general, and especially in the North of Ireland. To me, this indicated that the whole system of politics and governance must be fundamentally flawed if women did not want to get involved or couldn't get their foot in the door. I also wanted to go beyond the usual political questions and look at the stuff of real life. As far as I was concerned the Troubles had been the excuse for doing nothing about education, welfare, poverty, human rights and economic issues for 30 years. These areas were not even being considered because the 'constitutional question'[2] had not been answered!

I found out about the way the system of student representation worked. If you were a student in Northern Ireland you were automatically a member of both the National Union of Students in the UK, based in London, and of the Union of Students in Ireland, based in Dublin. Because USI was geographically more convenient, Northern Irish students tended to gravitate towards it. It's also fair to say that the

2 The question of whether Northern Ireland should be part of the United Kingdom or the Republic of Ireland.

students who made up the USI body understood more about our unique situation in the North.

My mates from the women's group, Lynn (the scary one), and Alison (the weird one), kept me up to date with the work of the USI. I was taken along to the annual Women's Congress, held in Dublin, and my mind was blown away. There were women students from all over Ireland and it was the most empowering feeling I'd ever had. Straight away I realised I wanted to be a part of it. The way to do that was to run for the Women's Rights Action Committee, or WRAC, so I stood up and said my name, and what college I was from. Then I just babbled. I couldn't help telling them all how bowled over I was at simply being there, and that I kept thinking about Annie and Aretha singing 'Sisters Are Doing It for Themselves'. And they elected me! This meant I got to go to meetings in Dublin to decide on different student policies, like childcare, political representation and so on.

It was amazing; a liberal, open-minded period of listening to women, rather than men who talked bullshit, empty vessels who enjoyed the sounds of their own voices. Now there was a fire in my belly and the following year, I was elected to the national executive of the USI as their Women's Rights Officer.

People often used to ask me why I bothered with student politics and the Union. Well, for one thing, it got me a job after I left university. Some people think all they need is a degree and they'll find a job no problem. That's rubbish. My involvement with student politics was an education independent of my academic studies and it gave me an edge over the rest.

I know people who graduated and had to take work in boring, hateful jobs. I got a chance to do something that I really wanted to do, which was to work with women around the issue of politics.

University is a place to discover your passions and find out who you are. University, and more importantly the experience I gained in the Union, turned my life around in more ways than one and it will always be a special place for me. It is also the place where I met my partner, with whom I now have a beautiful baby boy.

Bernadette

What Next?

Recently I was asked three troubling questions. They were put casually, but they caused a small explosion in my brain when I began to consider the answers. They were:

- What impact have the Troubles had on my life?
- What lessons have I learnt?
- What else is there?

I knew the answers were embedded somewhere within me, but I couldn't articulate them. I think I was almost afraid to let them out. What if they gave me away? What if they revealed me to be different in a place where we are taught from earliest childhood to cling to one identity or another?

I'm sure the Troubles must have made a huge difference to my life — it's just that the difference is almost impossible to identify. They've always been there, just on the edge. It's easy to become numb, almost to forget about them, to shut them out. Usually I didn't even react to reports of shootings or kneecappings. I do remember when a British soldier was shot dead about 100 yards from my school. I was totally apathetic. But then I could still be indignant and outraged when I learnt about the treatment of a friend's brother at the hands of the RUC. When it's someone you know, it's different.

My childhood memories are not dominated by stories of death and sacrifice, but about bringing in the hay in the summer, riding in the back of my father's truck with the wind in my face as he left his workmate home. Endless Saturdays filled with making camps out of old furniture and having pretend high-speed chases with my brothers and sisters in my parents' abandoned Peugeot.

Of course I remember the helicopters scaring me when they flew too low, the soldiers looking in the kitchen window at breakfast one morning and continually being stopped on the roads. But I accepted these things as normal, as only a child who knows nothing else can. So while the Troubles never had a direct influence in my life, they were always there in the background. For example I learnt a new word when my neighbour was murdered up the road and his wife put up a sign saying NO MEDIA. I had to ask my mother what media meant and thought myself very intelligent when she told me. I learnt the Republican songs (always handy on a night out); I picked up a few names and nicknames of weapons to impress foreigners. I learned nationalism and I learned to hate.

When I hit my teens I suddenly discovered 'The Cause' – the belief that there should be a united Ireland and that the British should cease all interference in Northern Ireland. I don't know how it happened exactly, but it came on me suddenly and fiercely. I jealously guarded my right to be Irish.

I spoke Gaelic as much as possible. I tripped off to the Gaeltacht and found like-minded youngsters and we immersed ourselves in our heritage (as well as revelling in the opportunities for drinking and meeting boys that present themselves when you're away from home for three weeks!). I made a half-hearted attempt to learn the tin whistle and a slightly more successful one at the boran.[1]

At that point I was even ready to die for my country. I was sure the Brits had to be met with violence. I remember coming face to face with a 12 July Orange parade on my way to work one summer's morning and being shocked at how strongly I felt the hatred rise in my throat towards the Protestant community. The thing was, I had these views but I'd never actually met any Protestants. I thought I hated all Prods; I thought they were all the same.

I began to devour history books about the 1916 Easter Rising and the beginning of 'The Struggle'. The Rising was the defining event of the Republican struggle against British rule, when a group of Irish nationalists rose up in Dublin, and for a short violent Easter weekend managed to hold off the British. The event probably would have passed from people's memories except that the authorities executed the rebel leaders, creating martyrs and incensing the Irish people.

As an angst-ridden teenager I was particularly drawn to this blood sacrifice ideal. I established a romantic, imagined attachment to the Rising's revolutionary leaders; I didn't want to let these forefathers and mothers down. I felt that they had literally given their lives for my freedom and I owed them. TV programmes and films such as 'Michael Collins' glamourised historical figures, making me feel proud to be Irish. They

---

1 A small, circular hand-held drum. A traditional Irish instrument.

seemed to justify the Troubles as a righteous struggle; Hollywood never supported the baddies.

I felt part of the fight, I belonged to a community – it was us against them – and it felt good. However, I didn't realise that I was being brainwashed; I was swallowing an ideology whole without questioning it, and I couldn't see the other side.

In the midst of my love affair with Irish heritage, I managed to pass my GCSEs and A levels. Suddenly I was in university – a new life, new people and new ideas. After nights out my friends and I would congregate and discuss the night's events. Inevitably the conversation would get round to 'the problem with Northern Ireland is...' For two months I argued till I was blue in the face for the God–given right to a United Ireland. Insisted that what our ancestors had given their lives for was not a wasted effort. I argued that we must be ready to carry on 'The Cause'. I then cemented my commitment by fully partaking in – and sometimes initiating – the drunken songs of oppression and freedom.

It was while attending a politics lecture at Queen's University that the ice began to melt – or rather crack – open. The 'political ideologies' module dissected all dogmas with a surgeon's knife: nationalism, feminism, fascism. When all emotion and passion was removed I was forced to look at a belief I had held dear.

That class was a catalyst that resulted in me challenging my own belief system. Slowly at first and then with continuing speed I realised that the glorious struggle was stupid, futile and ultimately tragic. I began to realise that my quest for a united land was not worth one drop of blood. That the Nationalist and Republican way I had revered for so long was merely a farce, a device to get votes and devotees.

I reacted strongly to this news, and for a while I rejected the whole notion of Irishness. I wanted to disassociate myself from a country that would allow its people to slaughter each other for a piece of land. Then I thought about who I was blaming – a country? That was ridiculous, the country was not real – it was a concept, a very cleverly constructed one, but just an idea all the same. It was dreamed up by a people long ago who wished to bind themselves to something, to belong. But now that idea has meant the murder of over 3000 people over many years and the spiral refused to stop because the enemies of logical thinking – rhetoric and propaganda – had become too powerful to control.

What else was there for me now that I had this disturbing knowledge? My arguments during our drunken ramblings had completely changed and yet I was unable to persuade anyone else of the truth of what I said. I began to wonder if my friends wanted to believe something different, or was their brain-washing complete? Over time, I have realised that 'truth' in Ireland is relative.

Growing up in South Armagh has shaped who I am. I still hold to most of the principles I grew up with, but these are tempered with an undestanding that they are not the only answer. I am still proud to be Irish, but I have a different understanding of what that means now. I can embrace my own cultural identity and accept other cultures too. Northern Ireland has shown me we need to keep changing – stagnant ideas are the real enemy, not each other. The Troubles have given me all the motivation I'll ever need to reach out to new people and new ideas.

Living in Northern Ireland has taught me many things; it has shown me that it doesn't really matter if we call it the North of Ireland or Northern Ireland. It has taught me that we must take our time to think and theorise. We have to find out who we are *now* and not continue to conform to the propaganda. We have to follow a new path. I sometimes think that is why the Troubles have continued for so long. We are so scared of having to find a new way and we continue on the old, not caring how many lives it costs because we are not sure if people will have the guts to let go.

In some ways, all of what I've said is the ramblings of a bored student. Everyone I know has his or her own opinion about 'the problem with Northern Ireland'. This is my take on the subject; these are my answers to the questions posed so casually.

Perhaps if everyone challenged themselves to answer the same questions we might get a little closer to letting go of all the baggage that we carry, all the propaganda and rhetoric, and begin to answer the fourth question: what's next?